# How To Stop Your Doctor Killing You

**What the papers say about Vernon Coleman and his books:**

'No thinking person can ignore him. This is why he has been for over 20 years one of the world's leading advocates on human and animal rights...Long may it continue!' *The Ecologist*

'Superstar.' *Independent on Sunday*

'Perhaps the best known health writer for the general public in the world today.' *The Therapist*

'The man is a national treasure.' *What Doctors Don't Tell You*

'Vernon Coleman writes brilliant books.' *The Good Book Guide*

'The revered guru of medicine.' *Nursing Times*

'A literary genius.' *HSL Newsletter*

'He's the Lone Ranger, Robin Hood and the Equalizer rolled into one.' *Glasgow Evening Times*

'Britain's leading health care campaigner.' *The Sun*

'Britain's leading medical author.' *The Daily Star*

'Brilliant.' *The People*

'Dr Vernon Coleman is one of our most enlightened, trenchant and sensible dispensers of medical advice.' *The Observer*

'The patient's champion.' *Birmingham Post*

'The medical expert you can't ignore.' *Sunday Independent*

'The most influential medical writer in Britain. There can be little doubt that Vernon Coleman is the people's doctor.' *Devon Life*

'The doctor who dares to speak his mind.' *Oxford Mail*

'Man with a mission.' *Morning News*

'Dr Coleman is more illuminating than the proverbial lady with the lamp.' *Company Magazine*

'Refreshingly sensible.' *Spectator*

'Dr Coleman gains in stature with successive books.' *Coventry Evening Telegraph*

'He writes lucidly and wittily.' *Good Housekeeping*

'The patient's champion. The doctor with the common touch.' *Birmingham Post*

'Clear and helpful.' *The Guardian*

'Vernon Coleman is a leading medical authority and known to millions through his writing, broadcasting and best selling books.' *Woman's Own*

'His message is important.' *The Economist*

'It's impossible not to be impressed.' *Western Daily Press*

'A persuasive writer whose arguments, based on research and experience, are sound.' *Nursing Standard*

'His book Bodypower' is one of the most sensible treatises on personal survival that has ever been published.' *Yorkshire Evening Post*

'Dr Coleman is crusading for a more complete awareness of what is good and bad for our bodies. In the course of that he has made many friends and some powerful enemies.' *Western Morning News*

'His advice is optimistic and enthusiastic.' *British Medical Journal*

'The calmest voice of reason comes from Dr Vernon Coleman.' *The Observer*

'A godsend.' *Daily Telegraph*


**A small selection from thousands of readers' letters:**

'I admire your forthright and refreshingly honest way of expressing your views and opinions...bless you for being a light in the eternal darkness.' *B. O.*

'If only more people in the medical profession and this government were like you it would be a much nicer world.' *G. W.*

'My deep appreciation for your great courage and integrity over the years.' *J. T.*

'Truly, truly, I greatly admire the work you have done for both animals and man. I think you are wonderful and I wish I had but half your mind power and courage.' *A. P.*

'I admire your direct approach and philosophy in respect of general health, especially sexual health, environmental and animal issues.' *A. W.*

'It's lovely to have someone who cares about people as you do. You tell us such a lot of things that we are afraid to ask our own doctors.' *K. C.*

'I would like to thank you for telling us the truth.' *R. K.*

'I feel I must write and congratulate you ... your no-nonsense attitude, teamed with plain common sense makes a refreshing change. Please keep up the good work.' *L.B.*

'Thanks over and over again – good health always to you as you are fighting for a good cause in life – for the sick.' *E.H.*

'I only wish to God that we had a few such as your good self in Parliament, then maybe our standard of life would possibly be better.' *H.H.*

'I must admit that initially I thought that some of your ideas were extreme, but sadly I must concede that I was wrong.' *C.D.*

'I greatly admire your no nonsense approach to things and your acting as champion of the people.' *L.A.*

'I have now read and studied all your excellent books and have enjoyed and benefited from them immensely.' *B.B.*

'May I say that I think you have done a real service to all those who have the sense and patience to study your books.' *B.A.*

## Books by Vernon Coleman

The Medicine Men (1975)
Paper Doctors (1976)
Everything You Want To Know About Ageing (1976)
Stress Control (1978)
The Home Pharmacy (1980)
Aspirin or Ambulance (1980)
Face Values (1981)
Guilt (1982)
The Good Medicine Guide (1982)
Stress And Your Stomach (1983)
Bodypower (1983)
An A to Z Of Women's Problems (1984)
Bodysense (1984)
Taking Care Of Your Skin (1984)
A Guide to Child Health (1984)
Life Without Tranquillisers (1985)
Diabetes (1985)
Arthritis (1985)
Eczema and Dermatitis (1985)
The Story Of Medicine (1985, 1998)
Natural Pain Control (1986)
Mindpower (1986)
Addicts and Addictions (1986)
Dr Vernon Coleman's Guide To Alternative Medicine (1988)
Stress Management Techniques (1988)
Overcoming Stress (1988)
Know Yourself (1988)
The Health Scandal (1988)
The 20 Minute Health Check (1989)
Sex For Everyone (1989)
Mind Over Body (1989)
Eat Green Lose Weight (1990)
Why Animal Experiments Must Stop (1991)
The Drugs Myth (1992)
How To Overcome Toxic Stress (1990)
Why Doctors Do More Harm Than Good (1993)
Stress and Relaxation (1993)
Complete Guide To Sex (1993)
How to Conquer Backache (1993)
How to Conquer Arthritis (1993)

Betrayal of Trust (1994)
Know Your Drugs (1994, 1997)
Food for Thought (1994, revised edition 2000)
The Traditional Home Doctor (1994)
I Hope Your Penis Shrivels Up (1994)
People Watching (1995)
Relief from IBS (1995)
The Parent's Handbook (1995)
Oral Sex: Bad Taste And Hard To Swallow? (1995)
Why Is Pubic Hair Curly? (1995)
Men in Dresses (1996)
Power over Cancer (1996)
Crossdressing (1996)
How to Conquer Arthritis (1996)
High Blood Pressure (1996)
How To Stop Your Doctor Killing You (1996, revised edition 2003)
Fighting For Animals (1996)
Alice and Other Friends (1996)
Spiritpower (1997)
Other People's Problems (1998)
How To Publish Your Own Book (1999)
How To Relax and Overcome Stress (1999)
Animal Rights – Human Wrongs (1999)
Superbody (1999)
The 101 Sexiest, Craziest, Most Outrageous Agony Column
       Questions (and Answers) of All Time (1999)
Strange But True (2000)
Daily Inspirations (2000)
Stomach Problems: Relief At Last (2001)
How To Overcome Guilt (2001)
How To Live Longer (2001)
Sex (2001)
How To Make Money While Watching TV (2001)
We Love Cats (2002)
England Our England (2002)
Rogue Nation (2003)
People Push Bottles Up Peaceniks (2003)

**novels**
The Village Cricket Tour (1990)
The Bilbury Chronicles (1992)
Bilbury Grange (1993)

Mrs Caldicot's Cabbage War (1993)
Bilbury Revels (1994)
Deadline (1994)
The Man Who Inherited a Golf Course (1995)
Bilbury Country (1996)
Second Innings (1999)
Around the Wicket (2000)
It's Never Too Late (2001)
Paris In My Springtime (2002)
Mrs Caldicot's Knickerbocker Glory (2003)

**short stories**
Bilbury Pie (1995)

**on cricket**
Thomas Winsden's Cricketing Almanack (1983)
Diary Of A Cricket Lover (1984)

**as Edward Vernon**
Practice Makes Perfect (1977)
Practise What You Preach (1978)
Getting Into Practice (1979)
Aphrodisiacs – An Owner's Manual (1983)
The Complete Guide To Life (1984)

**as Marc Charbonnier**
Tunnel (novel 1980)

**with Alice**
Alice's Diary (1989)
Alice's Adventures (1992)

**with Dr Alan C Turin**
No More Headaches (1981)

# How To Stop Your Doctor Killing You

**Vernon Coleman**

European Medical Journal

First published in 1996 by the European Medical Journal, Publishing House, Trinity Place, Barnstaple, Devon EX32 9HJ, England.

Revised edition published 2003

Reprinted 2004 (twice), 2005, 2006 (twice)

ISBN: 1 898947 14 7

A catalogue record for this book is available from the British Library.

Printed and bound by: 4word Ltd, Bristol.

'*Tell the truth, and you are likely to be ... a semi-criminal to authorities and damned with faint praise by your peers. So why do we do it? Because saying what you think is the only freedom.*'

ERICA JONG

# CONTENTS

Dedicated to my family of readers, who are a constant source of support and encouragement.

The person most likely to kill you is not a relative or a friend, or a mugger or a burglar or a drunken driver. The person most likely to kill you is your doctor. This book will show you how to look after yourself and to protect yourself from this serious threat to your life and good health.

## FOREWORD

### *Why, How And When Doctors Do More Harm Than Good*

Over the years the medical establishment has acquired a well deserved reputation for ignoring good discoveries (which would make a dramatic difference to human health) and continuing with useless practices (which do more harm than good) long after they should have abandoned them. The medical profession, or, perhaps I should say 'the medical establishment', has always been slow to accept and assimilate new ideas.

I have long thought that the main problem with modern medical education is that it is largely based upon learning by rote and upon eliminating all original thought. It only occurred to me recently that this is deliberate, since the aim of an orthodox modern medical education is to help maintain the status quo (and preserve the position of the pharmaceutical industry). Right from the very beginning young medical students are made to learn long lists of information. They learn the names of the bones, the arteries, the nerves and the veins in the body. They learn the names of the muscles and they learn the histology of the various organs. They then learn lists of clinical signs and symptoms. And they learn lists of drugs. At no point are students encouraged to think for themselves.

As a result it is not surprising that after graduation most doctors continue to do as they are told. The average doctor is strangely incapable of critical thought. Given the indoctrination they have undergone it is hardly surprising that doctors readily accept everything they are told by the drug companies (which more or less control post-graduate education) and equally readily reject alternative medicine – something which never made an appearance in the undergraduate syllabus and which cannot, therefore, be of any value.

(It also occurred to me recently that the authorities deliberately make formal medical education a lengthy business in order to make sure that by the time they qualify the vast majority of doctors will be nodding 'yes' men and women.)

Turning out doctors who are incapable of original thought, and who are unwilling to question the status quo, naturally means that our hospitals aren't renowned for developing new ideas. It also means that most GPs simply plod through their careers doing what the drug companies want them to do. This wouldn't matter too much if the doctors who aren't creative thinkers were reasonably receptive to original thinking from other people. But they aren't.

There is nothing new about this. The greatest thinkers – the ones who have, in the end, contributed most to medicine and human health – have always been scorned or ignored (or preferably both) by the medical establishment. The establishment has always manipulated the truth to suit its own political, religious or commercial purposes. Simple truths which are inconvenient have always been suppressed. It happened in the past, it will happen in the future and it happens now.

* * *

Few medical stories better illustrate the way the medical establishment works than the story of how scurvy was discovered, and how the treatment for it was ignored for centuries.

In 1535 Jacques Cartier sailed from France to Newfoundland with a crew of 110 men. Within six weeks a hundred of his men had developed scurvy. Luckily for Cartier and his men a native told them to drink the juice from the fruit of local trees. The men recovered in days. From that time on wise sea captains made sure that their men were given regular supplies of orange or lemon juice. In a book called *The Surgeons Mate*, published in 1636, John Woodall recommended that these juices be used to prevent scurvy. But the medical establishment was slow to accept this sensible suggestion. In 1747 the idea was reintroduced by James Lind, who conducted a proper clinical trial and proved that scurvy could be prevented with the right diet. It was Lind's work which enabled Captain Cook (he was a Lieutenant at the time) to sail around the world without a single case of scurvy.

The admiralty and the medical establishment continued to ignore all this. In the seven years war, from 1756 to 1763, approximately half of the 185,000 sailors involved died of scurvy. In 1779 the Channel Fleet had 2,400 cases of scurvy after a single ten week cruise.

Eventually, in 1795, the medical establishment (and the navy) succumbed to common sense and lemon juice became a compulsory part of every sailor's diet. (Hence the nickname 'limey' for a British sailor.) This breakthrough took well over two centuries to be accepted.

\* \* \*

There is no doubt that Paracelsus (Aureolus Theophrastus Bombastus von Hohenheim to his friends) is the father of modern medicine. He tore into the precepts of established medical thinking with all the zeal of a missionary. He revolutionised medical thinking throughout Europe and scandalised the medical establishment by claiming to have learned more from his contact with witches and midwives than from his study of ancient and well revered medical texts. No idea or theory was too bizarre to be studied and considered and no belief, no practice and no concept too sacred to be rejected. He was the first man to associate mining with chest disease, to use mercury in the treatment of syphilis, to advocate allowing wounds to drain instead of smothering them with layers of dried dung and to argue that some foods contained poisons which harmed the human body. Paracelsus scandalised the establishment by claiming that he was interested more in pleasing the sick than his own profession. He was, not surprisingly, rejected by the medical establishment and widely and persistently persecuted for beliefs. It was years after his death that his ideas were recognised. (Even today there are many within the medical establishment who still regard him as a renegade and a dangerous maverick.)

\* \* \*

In the 16th century, Andreas Vesalius achieved contemporary notoriety and eternal fame as the author of the first textbook of human anatomy, *De Humanis Corporis Fabrica*. Up until Vesalius, medical students had studied anatomy using texts prepared by Galen. Since Galen used pigs not human corpses for his studies his anatomical notes were, to say the least, rather misleading.

Vesalius's frank rejection of many of Galen's anatomical claims earned him considerable disapproval. The medical establishment still firmly believed that Galen could do no wrong. They weren't interested in anything as superficial and irrelevant as evidence.

Like so many original thinkers before and after him Vesalius was unable to cope with the outcry. He burnt his remaining manuscripts, abandoned his study of anatomy and took a job as court physician to Charles V in Madrid.

(Vesalius wasn't the only anatomist whose work was rejected. In the 17th century, British doctor William Harvey spent eight years researching the circulation of the blood – and getting it right. His patience was rewarded with ridicule. He received nothing but abuse. He lost many friends and his practice shrank.)

\* \* \*

When Ambrose Paré, the great French surgeon, first started work as an army surgeon it was accepted practice to stop a haemorrhage by sealing a wound with a red hot iron. Amputations were performed with a red hot knife and the wounds which were left were sealed with boiling oil. One day Paré ran out of boiling oil and used a mild emollient to dress the wounds of the men he was treating. He worried all night about what he had done but the next day he found that his patients were not only healthy but that they were also in less pain than the men whose wounds had been sealed with boiling oil. Paré was wise enough to learn from this and from that day on he started dressing wounds with an emollient rather than boiling oil. He also introduced ligatures, artificial limbs and many surgical instruments. Inevitably, Paré met the usual fate of innovators and reformers (who get a rougher ride within the world of medicine than anywhere else). He was denounced by other surgeons as dangerous and unprofessional. Older surgeons banded together to oppose him and in their attempts to discredit him they attacked him for all sorts of things – for example, his ignorance of Latin and Greek. Paré eventually succeeded because the soldiers he treated trusted him and wanted to be treated by him. They weren't interested in the views of the French medical establishment.

\* \* \*

When Tsar Paul came to power in Russia in 1796 he was so horrified at the state of the hospital in Moscow that he ordered it to be rebuilt. In Frankfurt in the 18th century physicians considered working in hospital to be equivalent to a sentence of death.

In 1788 Jacobus-Rene Tenon published a report on the hospitals of Paris which shocked city officials. He described how the Hotel Dieu (the magnificent looking hospital next to Notre Dame) contained 1200 beds but up to 7,000 patients – with up to six patients crammed into each bed. The stench in the hospital was so foul that people who entered would do so holding a vinegar soaked sponge to their noses. Very few patients escaped from the hospital with their lives. When reformer John Howard toured European hospitals he reported that no fresh air, no sunlight, straw as bedding, no bandages and a milk and water diet supplemented with weak soup were standard. The reports of Tenon and Howard were ignored and dismissed for years and it took decades for the medical establishment to make any real changes.

* * *

In the 18th century, the treatment of the mentally ill was abysmal. Daniel Defoe, best remembered for his story of the adventures of Robinson Crusoe wrote a vicious attack on mental hospitals. 'Is it not enough to make anyone mad,' he asked, ' to be suddenly clap'd up, stripp'd, whipp'd, ill fed and worse us'd? To have no reason assigned for such treatment, no crime alleged or accusers to confront? And what is worse, no soul to appeal to but merciless creatures who answer but in laughter, surliness, contradiction and too often stripes?' No one took much notice and medical practitioners continued to treat mentally ill patients without respect or care.

At the Bethlem Royal Hospital half-naked patients were kept chained in irons. Physicians bled their patients once a year and the more troublesome patients were put on a tranquillising wheel. Until 1770 visitors could pay a penny to see the 'fun' at Bedlam. John Wesley, founder of the Wesleyan Church, who considered himself a benefactor of the mentally ill, suggested pouring water onto the heads of the mentally ill and forcing them to eat nothing but apples for a month. Wesley was one of the first men to use electricity in the attempted treatment of the mentally ill. Despite the protests of reformers such as Philippe Pinel (who shocked the establishment in the late 18th century by claiming that the mentally ill were sick and needed treatment) mental hospitals were, well into the 19th century, still quite unsuitable for people needing medical treatment.

\* \* \*

There was never any evidence to show that it did any good but blood-letting was a favourite therapeutic tool for centuries. The fact that removing blood from a patient made him or her quieter was regarded as proof that it was doing some good. (This is no dafter than the rationale used to explain some modern treatments.) Blood-letting was easy to perform and it was something to do. Doctors have always felt the need to do something to their patients. (Possibly because it is difficult to explain away a big fee if all you do is give advice.) Leeches were hugely popular in the 19th century. In 1824 two million leeches were imported into France. In 1832 the figure had risen to 57 million a year.

\* \* \*

In 1843 the American poet, novelist and anatomist Oliver Wendell Holmes read to the Boston Society for Medical Improvement a paper entitled *On The Contagiousness of Puerperal Fever*. He argued that the disease could be carried from patient to patient by doctors. He suggested that surgeons should consider changing their clothes and washing their hands after leaving a patient with puerperal fever. His lecture annoyed the medical establishment and his advice was ignored completely. A similar fate befell Ignaz Philipp Semmelweiss who, in 1846, at the age of 28, became an assistant in an obstetric ward at the Allgemeines Krankenhaus in Vienna. Semmelweiss noticed that the number of women dying in his ward was higher than the number dying in other wards. It wasn't difficult to notice this. Women would beg, in tears, not to be taken into Semmelweiss's ward. Deciding that he wasn't that bad a doctor Semmelweiss looked for an explanation and came to the conclusion that the major difference was that patients on his ward were looked after by medical students whereas the patients on other wards were looked after by midwives. Semmelweiss then discovered that the students came straight to the ward from the dissecting room where they had had their hands stuck into the corpses of women who had died from puerperal fever. The midwives never went near to the dissecting room. Semmelweiss instructed the medical students that they should start washing their hands in a solution of calcium chloride after coming from the dissecting room. The remedy produced a dramatic drop in the death rate on his ward.

Predictably the medical establishment was not well pleased – even though Semmelweiss had proved his point very dramatically. The unfortunate young doctor couldn't cope with the rejection. He became an outcast and died in a mental hospital a few years later. The medical establishment had scored another hollow victory. Once again the patients were the losers.

\* \* \*

You might have thought that the medical establishment would have welcomed anaesthesia. After all, before anaesthetics were available, surgeons had to get their patients drunk or knock them out with a blow to the head. Surgeons would often operate with the patient held down by four strong men. The first operation under anaesthesia was performed at the Massachusetts General Hospital in 1846. But the establishment wasn't going to accept this new fangled nonsense lying down. The main objection was that anaesthetics were being used to help women who were in labour. And that, claimed the establishment, just wasn't acceptable. It was, said the wise men, unnatural and unhealthy for women to deliver babies without suffering pain. 'In sorrow thou shalt bring forth children,' says the bible. However, the religious barbarians were eventually overcome by Dr James Simpson who trumped the bible quoters with this quote: 'And the Good Lord caused a deep sleep to fall upon Adam and he slept; and He took one of his ribs and closed up the flesh instead thereof.' The opposition to anaesthesia was finally quelled when Queen Victoria gave birth to Prince Leopold while under the influence of chloroform.

\* \* \*

In 1867 Joseph Lister published a paper in *The Lancet* entitled *On the Antiseptic Principle in the Practice of Medicine*. Lister had found a solution to the age old problem of post-operative infection. But the medical establishment doesn't like change, even if it means keeping patients alive. And Lister found himself being attacked by doctors who ignored the evidence but disapproved of his new techniques simply because they were new. It was decades before the 'antiseptic principle' was accepted. (One of the reasons why hospital infections are so commonplace today is that doctors and nurses seem to believe that they can use antibiotics instead of washing their hands. Incompetence, carelessness and ignorance mean that the quality of cleanliness in the average modern hospital is little better than it was in a hospital in the middle ages.)

* * *

Until the 1980s it was common for surgery on babies to be performed without anaesthesia on the grounds that babies are incapable of feeling pain. There was no evidence for this claim (one which any mother would be able to oppose with credible if anecdotal evidence) but anaesthetists were taught that babies had immature nervous systems and so didn't need painkillers.

* * *

The medical establishment has always opposed original thought and protected the status quo – regardless of the effect on patients. My book *The Story of Medicine* is packed with examples illustrating the way that the medical establishment has acted in the interests of the profession but against the interests of patients and, later in this book, you'll find material describing when, how and why other imaginative, thoughtful and creative individuals have had a hard time.

The real tragedy is that absolutely nothing has changed. The medical establishment is still responsible for protecting medical procedures which do not work and have never worked (and which expose patients to great risk) while at the same time it opposes and suppresses treatments which do work and have been proved to work. Anyone who dares to offer warnings which don't fit in with the specific requirements of the medical establishment will get the Semmelweiss treatment.

For example, over the last thirty years I have published many warnings, most of them commercially inconvenient and many of them about particular pharmaceutical products or about the pharmaceutical industry in general. The medical establishment has always scoffed, sneered, ridiculed and done its best to suppress my warnings and ensure that they were ignored by others. In the beginning, medical spokesmen would openly laugh. These days they prefer to ignore my warnings and hope that no one will notice – they are, I suspect, becoming wary of my track record and aware that history is rather more on my side than theirs.

Below is a list of just a few of the warnings I have made since 1970, often years before anyone else – for example I was warning about the hazards of genetic engineering in the 1970s. In every case my initial warnings were dismissed as inaccurate, irrelevant or inconsequential by doctors, politicians and journalists. I wonder how many people died because the medical establishment preferred to protect industrial conglomerates rather than look after the interests of individual patients.

Although I was widely attacked by governments, the medical establishment and many parts of the media for making these warnings, the accuracy of many of the forecasts, predictions, exposés and warnings on the list is now widely accepted by the medical profession and the media.

1. Benzodiazepine tranquillisers such as Valium and Ativan can be addictive.
2. Passive smoking causes cancer.
3. Mobile phones (and masts) and power lines may cause cancer.
4. Tap water contains harmful drug residues.
5. Drug side effects are a major cause of illness and death.
6. Genetic engineering (in all its forms) can be a threat to human health.
7. Many patients can control their high blood pressure without drugs.
8. Although many medical screening programmes are profitable for doctors they are not much good to patients.
9. In the UK the quality of care within the National Health Service (NHS) varies enormously from area to area. Waiting lists in the NHS are kept artificially long by consultants anxious to boost their income from private patients.
10. Mad Cow Disease can affect humans. (And Mad Cow Disease is found in sheep.)
11. Warnings about the threat of AIDS to heterosexuals were wildly exaggerated. Far too much money has been wasted on AIDS – which may well not exist as a specific disease.
12. Tuberculosis is returning as a major threat.
13. The overuse of antibiotics causes superbugs and drug-resistant infections.
14. Deep vein thrombosis is one of many serious threats to air travellers.
15. Air conditioning systems can spread disease.
16. Doctors often treat patients with identical diseases in different ways.

17. Stress causes (or makes worse) over 90 per cent of illnesses.
18. Too much exercise is dangerous.
19. High technology medicine frequently does more harm than good.
20. Xenotransplantation (using animal organs for human patients) can be extremely hazardous.
21. The human body has extraordinary self-healing powers.
22. The power of the mind over the body is greatly under-estimated.
23. Antibiotics are wildly overused (by both doctors and farmers) with a consequential increase in the number of serious infections.
24. It is a myth that we are living longer than our ancestors.
25. One in six patients in hospital are there because they have been made ill by a doctor
26. Vaccination can be a major cause of illness. Vaccines are dangerous and cause many health problems – including autism. (I've been warning about vaccines for over 25 years.)
27. Anti-perspirants may be a health hazard to women.
28. Medical tests and investigations are frequently unreliable, unnecessary and harmful.
29. In my book *Paper Doctors* (1976) I explained why much modern medical research (particularly cancer research) is useless.
30. TENS machines are an excellent way to deal with pain.
31. X-rays are done too often – and cause illness.
32. Patients can benefit by learning to listen to their bodies.
33. Air-conditioning systems can be dangerous.
34. In 1988 I warned about the problems created by an ageing population.
35. Microwave ovens may be a health hazard.
36. Meat causes cancer. (Years ago I uncovered totally convincing – but widely suppressed – evidence. Meat is second only to tobacco as a cause of cancer.)
37. The reliance on animal experimentation is a significant factor in the incidence of doctor-induced illness.
38. Individuals who have damaged immune systems are more likely to develop cancer.
39. Asthma and depression are being wildly over-diagnosed by drug company controlled doctors who are keen to prescribe more pills.
40. Women who eat a high fat diet are more likely to get breast cancer.

41. Overweight individuals are more prone to cancer.
42. Women on Hormone Replacement Therapy may be more likely to develop breast cancer.

Those are just a few of the scores of warnings and predictions I've made – most of them one, two or three decades ago. When they were first made most of these warnings were received with laughter and derision by the medical establishment (and most medical journalists). Look through the list and you will see that many of these predictions and warnings have already been proved right. On many occasions the Government *eventually* acted on my recommendations. For example, when the Conservative Government changed the law about tranquilliser drugs the relevant Minister admitted at the Commons that they'd done it because of my columns. But it took 15 years of campaigning to force through the change.

* * *

Modern clinicians may use scientific techniques but in the way that they treat their patients they are still quacks and charlatans, loyal to existing and unproven ideas which are profitable, and resistant to new techniques and technologies which may be proven and effective. It is a fact that most medical procedures currently used have never been properly tested.

The fact that a doctor may use a scientific instrument in his work does not make him a scientist – any more than a typist who uses a word processor is a computer scientist. The scientific technology available to doctors may be magnificent but the application of the scientific technology is crude, untested and unscientific. Superstition and prejudice are commonplace in modern medicine. It isn't difficult to find examples illustrating the ineffectiveness of modern medical science.

If doctors used truly scientific methods when treating their patients they would happily use whichever form of treatment seemed to offer their patients the best chance of recovery. And they would use scientific methods to compare the effectiveness of orthodox methods (such as surgery, drugs and radiotherapy) with the effectiveness of unorthodox methods (such as diet).

Doctors do not do this.

When patients recover from cancer while or after receiving

orthodox medical therapy (usually one or more of the triumvirate of surgery, drugs or radiotherapy) doctors invariably claim that those patients have got better because of the therapy they have received. And, of course, any patient who survives for five years is said to have been cured. Doctors are always quick to claim the credit when they can.

However, doctors are far more sceptical when patients recover from 'alternative' or 'non-orthodox' remedies. When patients recover from cancer while or after receiving unorthodox therapy (such as a particular type of diet) they are usually said to have recovered 'in spite' of the treatment they have received. Patients who get better after unorthodox therapy are said to have been misdiagnosed or to have made an 'unexplained and spontaneous recovery'. (No patient in history has ever made an 'unexplained and spontaneous recovery' while or after receiving orthodox therapy). Patients who survive for five years after alternative therapy are said to be merely in remission, awaiting a relapse.

And although orthodox doctors are invariably derisive when alternative therapists write about individual patients, or describe isolated case histories, this is exactly what orthodox doctors themselves do. It is not at all uncommon for medical journals to contain articles and letters based upon experiences with one or maybe two patients. (I agree that these experiences may be valuable. What I object to is the hypocrisy of doctors rejecting anecdotal evidence produced by alternative practitioners.)

The medical establishment always tends to oppose anything new and original which threatens the status quo. When the disorder in question is as serious and as badly treated as cancer this arrogance and reluctance to even consider something new becomes rather close to deceit and professional recklessness. I could put forward a strong case to charge the medical establishment with manslaughter for its continued refusal even to acknowledge or investigate alternative methods of tackling cancer (methods which do not involve drugs, surgery or radiotherapy). The treatment methods offered by doctors are often the only methods patients know about, simply because other, less conventional approaches have either been totally suppressed or sneered at and derided so successfully that no one gives them any credence.

Most convincing of all, however, is the fact that practising physicians and surgeons invariably base their own treatment programmes upon their own personal experiences and upon their own (usually completely unscientific) views of what will be best for a particular patient.

For example, despite the availability of clear evidence showing the efficacy of diet, stress control and modest exercise in the treatment (as well as the prevention) of cardiac disease, most doctors still insist on treating all their heart patients with either surgery or drug therapy. And despite the existence of other, far more logical options, most doctors still insist that the only way to treat cancer is to attack it from the outside – rather than to help the body heal and protect itself.

If orthodox medicine was truly scientific then patients with the same symptoms would all receive the same treatment. They don't. There are almost as many different treatment programmes on offer as there are doctors in practice. If a patient who has been diagnosed as having a particular type of cancer visits three doctors, it's a pretty safe bet that he or she will be offered three quite different types of advice. Many 'official' anti-cancer programmes, accepted by the medical establishment, can reasonably be described as irrational and illogical. The survival of individual patients sometimes seems to be more a matter of luck than a matter of science. Doctors simply don't understand why when two patients are given a treatment one will die and one will live. It never occurs to them that there may be some other factor involved and that the death of one patient and the survival of the other may be quite unrelated to the medical treatment which was given.

The logical, scientific approach to any problem is always to tackle the cause rather than the symptoms. If your car has a leaky radiator hose it makes far more logical sense to replace the leaky hose than to keep on filling up the radiator with water. If your house roof is leaking it is far more logical to repair the roof than to put out a bucket to catch the drips.

Good doctors do sometimes follow this logical approach.

But, sadly, there are more bad doctors than good ones.

When the bad doctor sees a patient with indigestion he or she will simply prescribe an antacid remedy – knowing that it will temporarily relieve the patient's symptoms – and then send the patient away.

In contrast, when a good doctor sees a patient with indigestion he will want to find out what is causing the indigestion. He will investigate the patient's diet and other lifestyle habits in a search for a cause. And he will want to deal with the cause of the symptoms, rather than the symptoms themselves.

* * *

I am invariably described as 'controversial' for outlining these facts (anyone who tells the truth can expect to be described as 'controversial') but the figures proving that doctors are now a serious health hazard are incontrovertible. A study in the USA found that well over 100,000 people are killed by prescription drugs every year while over two million more suffer such severe side effects that they are permanently disabled or require long hospital stays. These figures don't include deaths or serious problems caused by misdiagnosis, surgical errors (such as the removal of the wrong organ or limb) or problems caused by unreadable handwriting on prescriptions.

Nor do these figures include the vast number of errors which are covered up. How many millions of patients are made ill by treatment and then told by their doctor that it is their original disease which is causing their symptoms? How many millions of grieving relatives are honestly told that their loved one died because he or she was killed by the treatment he was given?

Two Irish doctors reported in the *British Medical Journal* that 20 per cent of British patients who have slightly raised blood pressure are treated unnecessarily with drugs. A British Royal College of Radiologists Working Party reported that at least a fifth of radiological examinations carried out in National Health Service hospitals were clinically unhelpful. In Britain the Institute of Economic Affairs claimed that inexperienced doctors in casualty units kill at least one thousand patients a year.

Doctors now cause more serious illness than cancer or heart disease. One in six patients in hospital are there because they have been made ill by doctors. (If you want to see the evidence for this staggering but nevertheless entirely accurate assertion take a look at my book *Betrayal of Trust*.)

In America, the Public Citizen Health Research Group has shown that 'more than 100,000 people are killed or injured a year by negligent medical care'. The real figure is probably considerably higher than this and there can be little doubt that many of the injuries and deaths are caused by simple, straightforward incompetence rather than bad luck or unforeseen complications.

Many patients would undoubtedly be surprised (and horrified) to find out how many surgical procedures have never been properly tested, never been shown to be safe and never been shown to work.

* * *

It is when prescribing drugs – or giving vaccines – that I believe doctors do most harm.

According to the *Journal of the American Medical Association* the overall incidence of serious adverse drug reactions is now 6.7 per cent and the incidence of fatal adverse drug reactions is 0.32 per cent of hospitalised patients. *JAMA* estimates that in 1994 alone 2,216,000 hospitalised patients in the USA had serious adverse drug reactions and 106,000 had fatal adverse drug reactions. According to *JAMA* these figures mean that adverse drug reactions are now between the fourth and sixth leading cause of death in the USA. In compiling this data, *JAMA* excluded errors in drug administration, noncompliance, overdose, drug abuse, therapeutic failures and *possible* adverse drug reactions. Serious adverse drug reactions were defined as those which required treatment in hospital, were permanently disabling or resulted in death.

If drugs were only ever prescribed sensibly, and when they were likely to interfere with a potentially life-threatening disease, then the risks associated with their use would be acceptable. But all the evidence shows that doctors do not understand the hazards associated with the drugs they use and frequently prescribe inappropriately and excessively. Many of the deaths associated with drug use are caused by drugs which did not need to be taken.

It is now widely accepted that at least 40 per cent of all the people who are given prescription medicines to take will suffer uncomfortable, hazardous or potentially lethal side effects. I say 'at least' because, for a variety of reasons, the vast majority of doctors never admit that their patients ever suffer any side effects. In Britain, for example, five out of six doctors have never reported any drug side effects to the authorities – authorities who admit that they receive information on no more than 10 – 15 per cent of even the most serious adverse drug reactions occurring in patients. In other words they admit that they never hear about at least 85 – 90 per cent of all dangerous drug reactions!

Astonishingly, it is even accepted that some doctors will withhold reports of serious adverse reactions and keep their suspicions to themselves in the hope that they may later be able to win fame by publishing their findings in a journal, or revealing their discovery to a newspaper or magazine.

Because the real figures about drug hazards are hidden most patients assume that all prescribed drugs are safe to take, will act in a predictable, effective way and are of recognised quality and standard. None of these assumptions is correct. Patients who take drugs are taking a risk; they are often taking part in a massive experiment and by taking a medicine may become worse off than if they had done nothing. To make things worse no one knows exactly how big the risks are when a particular drug is taken. Drugs are potential poisons that may heal or may kill.

The medical profession, the drug industry and the regulatory bodies all accept that the hazards of using any drug will only be known when the drug has been given to large numbers of patients for a considerable period of time.

Astonishingly, despite the hazards associated with their use, drugs are controlled less in their development, manufacture, promotion, sale and supply than virtually any other substance imaginable – with the exception of food.

In an average sort of year in a developed country at least 1 in 250 people will be admitted to hospital because of a drug overdose. One in 50 of them will die. That's bad. But even more worrying is the fact that every day thousands of people are admitted to hospital not because of an overdose but because a drug taken at prescribed levels has caused serious and possibly life-threatening symptoms.

One of the major reasons for the disastrously high incidence of problems associated with drug use is the fact that the initial clinical trials, performed before a drug is made available for all general practitioners to prescribe for their patients, rarely involve more than a few thousand patients at most. Some initial trials may involve no more than half a dozen patients.

However, it is now well known that severe problems often do not appear either until at least 50,000 patients have taken a drug, or until patients have used a drug for many months or even years. Because of this a huge death toll can build up over the years. Drug control authorities admit that when a new drug is launched no one really knows what will happen or what side effects will be identified.

Doctors and drug companies are, it seems, using the public in a constant, ongoing, mass testing programme. And the frightening truth is that far more people are killed as a result of prescription drugs than are killed as a result of using illegal drugs such as heroin or cocaine.

The treatments for many common diseases such as arthritis, backache and allergies such as hay fever and eczema frequently provide inadequate relief and often cause adverse effects which are far worse than the original complaint.

Although the drug industry can be blamed for failing to perform adequate tests on the drugs which they put on the market it is only doctors who can be blamed for overprescribing and for the inappropriate prescribing of drugs.

Doctors are now a public menace of phenomenal proportions. A study in Australia showed that 470,000 Australian men, women and children are admitted to hospital every year because they have been made ill by doctors. The figures also show that every year 280,000 patients who are admitted to hospital suffer a temporary disability as a result of their health care. Around 50,000 of these suffer permanent disabilities. A staggering 18,000 Australians die annually as a result of medical errors, drug toxicity, surgical errors and general medical mismanagement. What a terrible indictment of the medical profession. In America the death rate from medical 'accidents' is running at around 200,000 a year. Figures in Europe are no better. Doctors kill far, far more people than breast cancer or, indeed, most other types of cancer. When I mentioned in a radio broadcast that one in six patients in hospital are there because they have been made ill by a doctor, a representative of the medical establishment did not try to argue the point but merely pointed out, with apparently genuine pride and absolutely no sense of the absurd, that this at least meant that five out six patients in hospital were *not* there because they had been made ill by a doctor. (No, I could hardly believe it either. But I listened to a tape of the programme afterwards, and that is exactly what he said.) Not even members of the medical establishment can deny that doctors are a major cause of illness and death – well above all other forms of accidents combined, and ranking alongside cancer and heart disease.

* * *

It's genuinely difficult to know where to start (or stop) when trying to work out why doctors now do so much harm.

Some of the shortcomings are very basic. Most doctors simply don't listen properly to their patients. They hear a symptom, reach for the prescription pad and scribble out a pharmacological solution. Prescribing a drug has become a reflex. Take away a doctor's prescription pad and he will be helpless. Most doctors also fail to ask the right questions. They behave as though they are simply marketing men for the pharmaceutical industry; scribbling away their lives, and their patients' lives, to ensure that the industry which owns the medical establishment continues to thrive and make enormous profits.

Most patients probably assume that when a doctor proposes to use an established treatment to conquer a disease he will be using a treatment which has been tested, examined and proven. But this is not the case.

A few years ago the *British Medical Journal* reported that there are 'perhaps 30,000 biomedical journals in the world, and that they have grown steadily by 7 per cent a year since the 17th century.' The editorial also reported that: 'only about 15 per cent of medical interventions are supported by solid scientific evidence' and 'only 1 per cent of the articles in medical journals are scientifically sound'.

What sort of science is that? How can doctors possibly regard themselves as practising a science when six out of seven treatment regimes are unsupported by scientific evidence and when 99 per cent of the articles upon which clinical decisions are based are scientifically unsound?

Most medical research is organised, paid for, commissioned or subsidised by the drug industry. This type of research is designed, quite simply, to find evidence showing a new product is of commercial value. The companies which commission such research are not terribly bothered about evidence; what they are looking for are conclusions which will enable them to sell their product. Drug company sponsored research is done more to get good reviews than to find out the truth.

The other type of research that is done is the sort which is done by doctors or scientists wishing to advance their careers. All young doctors and medical scientists who wish to progress within the medical establishment must publish as many scientific papers as possible.

The real, unstated reason for many medical theses and papers is that they give appointments committees something to measure. But is this a criterion which commends itself to the general public who pay for our services? Would you prefer your treatment to be supervised by a physician who had published 15 papers rather than 14?

A general practitioner claims that she was told by a fellow doctor: 'Find something to measure, and then keep on measuring it until you can put six points on a graph. Then start submitting abstracts, because you'll soon be applying for senior registrar jobs and you'll need at least 10 publications to get on the shortlist.' The GP claims that the registrar who told her this also said: 'Look, I'll help you out a bit. I'll put your name on everything I publish from this lab if you put my name on everything you publish.'

Those scientists who still do original and unsponsored research might claim that their work is of potential value but the evidence contradicts that view.

Even more worrying is the fact that there is now a considerable amount of evidence to show that many modern so-called scientists are prepared to 'alter' their results if their experiments do not turn out as planned. (This cavalier attitude towards scientific experiments may well have been acquired from the world's drug companies – which have a well deserved reputation for amending or suppressing unsatisfactory results).

It is perhaps not surprising that it is now reliably estimated that at least 12 per cent of scientific research is fraudulent.

* * *

The tests and investigations which doctors use to help them make diagnoses are also unreliable and the likelihood of a doctor accurately predicting the outcome of a disease is often no more than 50:50.

Two pathologists carried out 400 post-mortem examinations and found that in more than half the patients the wrong diagnosis had been made. This presumably also means that in more than half the patients the wrong treatment had been given. And since modern treatments are undeniably powerful it also presumably means that a large proportion of those patients may have died not because of their disease but because of their treatment. The two pathologists reported that potentially treatable disease was missed in one in seven patients. They found that 65 out of 134 cases of pneumonia had gone unrecognised while out of 51 patients who had suffered heart attacks doctors had failed to diagnose the problem in 18 cases.

The sad truth is that the modern clinician does not put his treatments to the test and does not want to put his treatments to the test. Indeed, if it is suggested that he expose his treatment methods to a true, scientific analysis he will throw up his hands in horror, arguing that it would be unethical to test his treatments for that might deprive his patients of help. He will argue that his treatments do not need to be tested because he knows that they work. Today's medical training is based upon pronouncement and opinion rather than on investigation and scientific experience. In medical schools students are bombarded with information but denied the time or the opportunity to question the ex-cathedra statements which are made from an archaic medical culture. The drugs and tools which are used may be devised with the aid of scientific techniques but the way in which they are used is certainly not scientific.

If medicine was a science then when a patient visited a doctor complaining of a symptom he would be given the best, proven treatment, a treatment that was quite specific for the disease. Treatments for specific symptoms would be predictable and diagnostic skills would, because they would be based on scientific techniques, be reliable within certain acknowledged limits. But that is not what happens at all. In some areas of medicine specialists operate in a way that would be considered a variety of pseudoscience if the practitioners did not happen to have qualifications recognised by the medical establishment.

* * *

Here, just for the record, are some of the specific errors modern doctors make. These are the modern equivalents of putting the mentally ill on the tranquillising wheel; the modern equivalents of bleeding the sick and the restless in order to mask their symptoms and drown their complaints.

1.  Doctors rely too much on high-tech equipment for making diagnoses. They forget that high-tech testing and diagnostic equipment can often be fallible and that common sense is a grossly under-estimated weapon in a physician's diagnostic armoury. Too often it is the test result which is treated, rather than the patient.

2. Modern doctors are addicted to prescribing. They forget (if they ever knew) that the basic needs of the human body are fresh air, fresh drinking water, good food, regular exercise, plenty of sunshine, a little peace occasionally, and an acceptable environmental temperature. Instead, doctors rely heavily (almost totally) on drugs which are often ineffective and frequently dangerous. Doctors (led by the drug industry) like to believe that they have been responsible for improving the quality of our health – and life expectation. They're wrong. Clean water supplies, efficient sewage disposal, the telephone and central heating have all had a greater impact on our health than the entire medical establishment. Penicillin and X-rays, arguably the two most dramatic and significant medical discoveries of all time, were both discovered by accident. Neither of those discoveries were made by medical practitioners.

3. The medical establishment says that vaccines are good. And so doctors jab away, encouraged by the fact that they get paid well for every vaccination they give and (in the UK at least) have to pay a financial forfeit if they fail to vaccinate a high enough percentage of their patients. (I wonder how many patients know that when doctors recommend vaccination they do so because the more they vaccinate the bigger their annual bonus will be.).

4. Doctors constantly fail to assess new technologies and drugs before making them widely available. New surgical techniques are often put into practice without there being any evidence to show that they are safe or effective. And many drugs are put on the market – and made available to millions of patients – before they have been proved to be effective and safe. It is constantly surprising to find out just how little research is done into fundamental medical practices. For example, the other day I tried, unsuccessfully, to find evidence showing that dental flossing is safe and effective. Doctors and dentists recommend flossing but no one, it seems, has bothered to do any research to find out whether flossing damages the gums (causing bleeding and then forcing bacteria into the tiny cuts) or helps remove debris and keep gums healthy.

5. Because the medical establishment is owned by the pharmaceutical

industry doctors steadfastly refuse to acknowledge alternative remedies which can often be safer and more effective than orthodox remedies.

6.　Doctors remain woefully ignorant about the principles of healthy eating. Most doctors give little or no advice on food. When they do give advice it is often terrible. To give just one example, most doctors still don't realise that meat and fatty food are major causes of cancer. (When you realise that, just a few years ago, most doctors surveyed didn't know that tobacco was a major cause of cancer this is not quite such a surprise.)

7.　The importance of the mind in creating and preserving a healthy body is widely ignored and underestimated. Most doctors receive very little training in mental health and have little or no understanding of stress. Most doctors don't understand how and why patients may be able to deal with health problems (such as high blood pressure) by learning how to relax.

8.　Doctors still do far too much surgery – even though the evidence shows that much surgery is unnecessary. The hysterectomy operation is done far too often. Tonsils are frequently removed unnecessarily. One of the biggest money spinning operations for surgeons these days is heart surgery. But heart surgery isn't the best way to tackle serious heart disease. In addition doctors also commonly make the mistake of doing surgery at the wrong times. There is clear evidence to show that a woman's chances of responding well to surgery will depend on the time in her menstrual cycle that the surgery takes place.

9.　Doctors rely far too much on research which has involved the use of animals. Doctors who rely on animal experiments are misled by inaccurate information and end up giving bad advice and bad treatment to their patients. The evidence shows clearly that animal experiments are worthless and are a hazard to human health.

10.　The medical profession still ignores preventive medicine. It is now pretty well accepted that 80 per cent of cancers could be avoided. Cancer deaths remain high because doctors still do not accept this proven truth. How many doctors are warning about the hazards which may be associated with microwave ovens, mobile telephones, television sets, hospital food, genetic engineering and cramped aeroplanes with poor air conditioning systems?

\* \* \*

The inescapable conclusion from all this evidence is that today's doctors and nurses should carry a health hazard warning stamped on their foreheads. Each hospital should have a health warning notice hung over its entrance.

But our politicians – terrified of taking on the medicine 'industry' – have done nothing to try to improve the quality of care provided to patients. The politicians have bent over backwards to keep the drug industry happy. Governments do nothing to protect patients.

The incidence of doctor-induced illness is now epidemic throughout the western world. A high proportion of the patients in hospital are there because of some side effect of their medication. It is impossible to quantify the overall size of the problem precisely – particularly in general practice – for the very simple reason that the vast majority of doctors just don't bother to record or report drug side effects (even though the evidence shows that 40 per cent of patients suffer side effects while taking drugs). But there is no doubt that doctor-induced illness is now one of (if not the) greatest cause of illness in most so-called 'developed' countries. Well over a million patients a year are admitted to English hospitals because they have been made ill by doctors.

Patients should not trust the medical establishment but should be prepared to look outside the establishment to find the best, safest and most effective treatment programmes.

You should be extremely wary about your doctor. Remember that his motives (financial gain and professional status) may not be the same as yours (pain free survival).

\* \* \*

Most people recognise the damage that other doctors can do but like to think that *their* doctor is an honourable exception. This is entirely understandable. After all, we all like to think that our relationship with our own doctor is special and that we have chosen someone reliable and knowledgeable to look after us. We like to think of our doctor as a personal and family friend. We all need to put some trust in the health care professionals upon whom we rely when we are ill.

But it is just as dangerous to assume that *your* doctor is entirely safe, sensible, knowledgeable, competent and error free as it would be to assume that you do not need to take care when driving, on the spurious grounds that road accidents only ever affect other people.

You probably make some effort to ensure that the tyres on your car have plenty of tread, that the brakes are in good, working condition, that you wear a seat belt and so on. Everyone knows that motor cars can kill and so sensible individuals do what they can to protect themselves.

And yet more than four times as many people a year die as a result of medical 'accidents' as die as a result of road accidents. Put another way this means that your doctor is four times as likely to kill you as your car. In the last few decades doctors and hospitals around the world have killed more people than Hitler.

Even good, kind, conscientious doctors – who are honest and honourable, who care about their work and who do their very best for their patients – can still make people ill. And can still kill people.

For example, many of the problems caused by doctors are a result of prescription drug consumption. When he writes out a prescription your doctor has to rely upon the honesty and integrity of the drug company making the product he is prescribing. And, since most drug companies do not operate in an honest way, that is a fundamental error of trust which can lead to many problems. You suffer from his trust in the drug company.

To that you must add the fact that all patients are individual and different. A drug which has proved effective and safe when given to 99 or 999 patients may still prove dangerous and deadly when given to the 100th or the 1000th patient. Every patient who takes a drug – even a well tried drug – is participating in an experiment. Most doctors either do not understand this or they forget it in the heat of daily practice.

The bottom line is that however good your doctor is – and however much you may trust him or her – you must share the responsibility for your own health and you must know when to tell your doctor if you think that the treatment with which he or she is providing you could be causing problems.

* * *

There is nothing new in the fact that doctors kill people. Doctors have always made mistakes and there have always been patients who have died as a result of medical ignorance or incompetence.

But, since we now spend more on health care than ever before, and since the medical profession is apparently more scientific and better equipped than ever before, there is a savage irony in the fact that we have now reached the point where, on balance, well-meaning doctors in general practice and highly trained, well-equipped specialists working in hospitals do more harm than good. The epidemic of iatrogenic disease which has always scarred medical practice has been steadily getting worse and today most of us would, most of the time, be better off without a medical profession.

Most developed countries now spend around eight per cent of their gross national products on health care (the Americans spend considerably more – around 12-14 per cent) but through a mixture of ignorance, incompetence, prejudice, dishonesty, laziness, paternalism and misplaced trust doctors are killing more people than they are saving, and they are causing more illness and more discomfort than they are alleviating.

Most developed countries now spend around one per cent of their annual income on prescription drugs and doctors have more knowledge and greater access to powerful treatments than ever before, but there has probably never been another time in history when doctors have done more harm than they do today. I doubt if anyone knows just how much damage the overprescribing of drugs and vaccines (many of which are of dubious value) does to the human immune system. My personal view is that all those prescription drugs have had, are having, and are likely to continue to have, a devastating effect on human health.

It is true, of course, that doctors save thousands of lives by, for example, prescribing life-saving drugs or by performing essential life-saving surgery on accident victims.

But when the medical profession, together with the pharmaceutical industry, claims that it is the advances in medicine which are responsible for the fact that life expectancy figures have risen in the last one hundred years or so they are dead wrong.

Orthodox medical practitioners like to give the impression that they have conquered sickness with science but there are, at a conservative estimate, something in the region of 18,000 known diseases for which there are still no effective treatments – let alone cures.

As drug companies become increasingly aware that curing serious disease is beyond their capability (and, indeed, their desire – for why should drug companies, which make their money out of people being sick, want to make people well?), they spend more and more effort on finding drugs to improve life or performance in some vague way.

There can be little doubt that a former Director General of the World Health Organisation got it absolutely right when he startled the medical establishment by stating that 'the major and most expensive part of medical knowledge as applied today appears to be more for the satisfaction of the health professions than for the benefit of the consumers of health care'.

The evidence certainly supports that astonishing and apparently heretical view. Profits, not patients, are now the driving force which rule the medical profession's motives, ambitions and actions. Doctors don't seem to care any more. The passion has gone out of medicine.

In my view the biggest single reason why the medical profession is killing so many people is its alliance with the pharmaceutical industry.

The myth that we live long and healthy lives thanks to the drug industry and the medical profession has increased our expectations. We no longer expect to fall ill. We expect a magic solution when we fall ill. We don't want to be bothered making any effort to stay healthy because we have been taught to have faith that if we fall ill then the medical men will be able to cure us.

The majority of illnesses do not need drug treatment. Most patients who visit a doctor neither want nor expect drug treatment. But at least eight out of ten patients who visit a general practitioner will be given a prescription (though growing numbers of patients do not take the drugs that are prescribed for them).

As I have shown in numerous previous books (for example *How To Live Longer*) we aren't living longer than our ancestors and we certainly aren't fitter than them either. We do not live healthier lives than our predecessors. On the contrary, although we consume greater and greater quantities of medicine than ever before, more of us are ill today than at any time in history. On any day you care to choose in just about any developed country you care to mention over half the population will be taking a drug of some kind. A recent survey of 9,000 Britons concluded that one in three people are suffering from a long standing illness or disability. Other surveys have shown that in any one fourteen day period 95 per cent of the population consider themselves to be unwell for at least a few of those days. At no time in history has illness been so commonplace. We spend more than ever on health care but no one could argue that there is any less suffering in our society.

* * *

These are difficult, 'interesting' times. Doctors, whom we pay to look after our health, seem to be determined to kill us all as quickly and as painfully as they can. And politicians, whom we pay to protect us from those who wish us ill, have forgotten all about 'duty' and 'responsibility' (even the words now seem rather quaint and old-fashioned) and, instead, concentrate their efforts on power and money. Make no mistake, your Government wants you dead at 65 because after that you will just be a liability. Your Government is not going to protect you against the bad guys.

You can no longer rely on being able to obtain skilled and reliable medical help.

The answer is to learn how to look after yourself; and to learn when you can (and cannot) trust doctors with your life.

*Vernon Coleman 2003*

## Introduction To The Original Edition

No one knows precisely how many people are killed every year by doctors

Not surprisingly, the medical profession isn't too keen on sharing that sort of information with patients.

This is partly because they don't want to scare too many people away by broadcasting the truth. After all, orthodox medicine is, these days, in close competition with many varieties of alternative medicine and doctors are only too well aware that their safety record is considerably worse than any of the competitors.

But this shyness is also a result of a perhaps understandable reluctance to share information that could lead to doctors spending even more of their time in court than they do at the moment.

As I showed in my book *Betrayal of Trust* one in six patients who are in hospital are there because they have been made ill by a doctor. This figure is, if anything, an under-estimate. Given half a chance most doctors will write 'cardiac failure' or 'pneumonia' on the death certificate rather than the possibly more honest 'medical cockup'.

Most of the world's medical profession studiously ignored the revelations in *Betrayal of Trust*, despite the importance of the evidence and the fact that I was claiming – and substantiating – that, on balance, doctors now do more harm than good and are as important a cause of illness and death as heart disease and cancer.

I don't think any doctor has ever disputed my claim that one in six patients in hospital are there because they have been made ill by doctors. But many doctors seemed unhappy about the fact that I was saying it in public. A not uncommon complaint was that I was bringing the profession into disrepute by giving the public this sort of information.

I felt the implication was that the world would be better served if I would shut up, go away and let the people who know best (the medical profession) look after things.

Doctors do not kill patients (nor even make them ill) because they are particularly evil, mean-spirited or psychopathic. Most doctors are quite decent people. Their motives are honest enough; they want to make a good living doing a useful job. There are evil, mean-spirited and psychopathic doctors around, of course. But no more than you would find among accountants, solicitors or estate agents.

Doctors kill patients (and make them ill) for two main reasons. The first is that many are, generally speaking, professionally incompetent.

The interview is the most important part of the doctors diagnostic equipment. That's when he talks to the patient and – even more important than talking, though you wouldn't think so if you sat in on the average out-patients' clinic – listens to what the patient has to say. It is by talking and listening to patients that doctors learn most.

Over the years doctors have accumulated more and more equipment. But, instead of helping, the equipment has come between the doctor and the patient. Too often the doctor relies exclusively on his equipment; trusting it implicitly to provide him with the right answers. And all too often the result is that he produces an ill-fitting off-the-peg diagnosis rather than a bespoke diagnosis which can lead to appropriate and effective treatment.

The first piece of equipment that doctors acquired was the stethoscope. This now symbolic device was invented so that doctors could listen to their patients' chests without having to put their heads down on their bosoms. The stethoscope added to the doctor's dignity. But it also provided the first mechanical barrier between doctor and patient. And since René Laennec first introduced the stethoscope the doctor patient relationship has been weakened and damaged by the obsession with equipment, and the failure to respect the relationship between doctor and patient.

A few years ago, an American study showed that one person in ten who had died would have still been alive if the doctors looking after them had relied upon their heads instead of their equipment.

One problem is the fact that the equipment doesn't allow for individual eccentricities – and the reality that your body might be slightly different to mine.

Things are made even worse by the fact that equipment often breaks down and is frequently badly maintained. Shops have to have their scales calibrated but ask your doctor when he last had his blood pressure machine calibrated and watch him blush.

Can you think of any reason why the thousands of pieces of equipment which are supplied to hospitals should be any more reliable than the equipment you buy for the kitchen? I believe that as much as half of the new equipment being delivered to hospitals could be defective.

If that doesn't worry you then the fact that many of the doctors who are responsible for using the equipment don't know how it works, how it should be calibrated or how to tell if it is working properly, should worry you.

The second reason why doctors kill so many people is that they are politically innocent and commercially inept and nowhere near as bright or as street-wise as they would like the rest of the world to think they are.

Through a mixture of ignorance and stupidity they do not realise that the profession of which they are, largely, proud members has been sold to the pharmaceutical industry by the international medical establishment.

Whether the medical profession has sold out to the pharmaceutical industry because it is populated by greedy, grasping and unscrupulous men and women or because it is full of individuals who are politically innocent and commercially inept is difficult to say. My suspicion is that doctors around the world are so full of their own self-importance and so out of touch with reality that they do not even realise that they have been bought and are now controlled by the world's most unscrupulous industry.

* * *

Back in the middle ages people were reluctant to go into hospital. They knew that they were unlikely to get out alive. Those patients who survived the incompetent ministrations of doctors and nurses were likely to die of infections contracted on the ward.

Things didn't get much better until well into the twentieth century when the discovery of anaesthetics, antiseptics and antibiotics gradually meant that patients going into hospital had a reasonable chance of benefiting from the experience.

But the good days are now over. Modern medicine has again become a major hazard. And doctors are again one of the most significant causes of death and ill health.

Politicians must undoubtedly take some of the blame for this disastrous state of affairs. It is, after all, they who have handed over control of our hospitals to an ever growing and increasingly incompetent bureaucracy.

In many countries both the number of nurses working in hospitals and the number of beds available for patients have been falling steadily for years. But at the same time the number of administrators employed has been rising remorselessly. In the UK there are now more administrators than beds in NHS hospitals. Wards are closed down or lie unused and empty while administrators spend essential funds which could be used for looking after patients on wall-to-wall carpeting, exotic pot plants and weekend conferences in expensive locations. Changing a light bulb costs a small fortune in administrative costs and it can take so long to persuade five administrators to send along one electrician that I've known nurses take in their own light bulbs and surreptitiously change them themselves. It is so much quicker and easier than filling in all the necessary forms.

We can blame the administrators for failing to administer hospitals and healthcare properly but we must blame the politicians for giving them the power they are now abusing.

* * *

But although the politicians and the administrators waste money and resources, and have undoubtedly weakened health services, it isn't solely their fault that doctors and hospitals now do more harm than good. Orthodox medicine has become a menace to patients because the medical establishment has sold itself – body and soul – to the drug industry.

If you're naive and innocent you probably imagine that when a doctor decides to prescribe a drug for you he selects a product which independent research has shown to be most effective for your condition.

He doesn't. Most doctors probably wouldn't know what to do with independent research if they saw it. When the doctor reaches for his pen and his pad he writes out a prescription for a drug about which he knows only what he has been told by the drug company's representative or what he has read in the drug company's advertisements.

The savage truth is that medicine is no longer a profession. Today's doctors are merely a marketing arm of the pharmaceutical industry. Doctors, once a responsible and respectable group of men and women, have sold their souls for an endless supply of free meals, free pens and free golf balls.

When it comes to honest and reliable advertising the drug companies come a long way after second-hand car salesmen. The drug companies – and their vastly overpaid executives – will do anything to make money. These people are so ruthless that they make the Colombian drug barons look like boy scouts. Much of the stuff doctors prescribe is complete rubbish. Most of it has never been shown to be either safe or effective. Drug companies test the stuff they sell on animals (proven to be entirely useless for predicting what will happen when pills are given to people) and then ruthlessly use the sort of techniques usually employed to sell shampoo, cigarettes, cars and perfume to naive and innocent punters to persuade doctors to contribute to their profits.

As a final insult to the patient, if politicians dare to hint that they are unhappy about paying inflated prices for pharmaceutical junk that doesn't work, the pharmaceutical companies simply threaten to take their pill producing factories and their massive profits off to some other country where the politicians know enough to treat drug company executives with the respect they require.

Politicians, bureaucrats and doctors have put health care back into the middle ages.

* * *

The purpose of this book is simple: to encourage you to be sceptical of your doctor, to teach you what to watch out for (and how your doctor may make you ill) and to show you how to stay healthy so that you will be less likely to need to come into contact with any health care professional.

I have been a passionate advocate of patient consumerism for over two decades and the pages which follow are packed with advice and tips on how you can live a longer, healthier life – and protect yourself from an increasingly incompetent and dangerous medical profession. Apart from being aware of the threat to your health that your doctor poses (and if you want to stay alive and healthy you should treat all doctors and other health professionals with a considerable amount of suspicion) you should learn to take control of your own life as much as possible. You should learn to be independent and sceptical. You should ask the right questions (this book will tell you the questions to ask) and, most crucial of all, retain overall responsibility for your health. You should know what to watch out for when taking drugs (this book will tell you what to watch out for) and you should know how to be an independent, sceptical consumer. And you should know how to use – and get the best out of – doctors and hospitals when you do need them.

*Vernon Coleman, 1996*

## 1  Don't Let Your Doctor Bully You

Doctors used to be trusted and respected by their patients. But, sadly, that's not always true these days.

Gradually, doctors have become more and more unpopular. I don't think this has got anything to do with the treatments doctors offer – or with the effectiveness or otherwise of their cures. I think that the reason is much simpler. Doctors are unpopular today because they are offhand, patronising and bloody rude. They treat patients without respect and bully them into submission.

Every day I get letters from patients who have been treated like dirt when they've dared to ask questions or speak out of turn.

'I was in tears when I left the hospital,' complained one reader. 'The consultant kept me waiting for three hours then hardly spoke to me. When he'd finished poking and prodding he just walked away. A nurse came and told me I could leave. My husband, who was waiting outside for me wanted to go in and punch him. I still don't know what's wrong with me.'

I sometimes feel ashamed to be a member of the medical profession.

'I was taken into a cold examination room and told to take off all my clothes and lie on a couch,' wrote another patient. 'I was left there, naked, for 25 minutes. I was sitting on the couch hugging my knees to keep warm when the consultant, a nurse and a trail of medical students burst into the room. The doctor then gave me an internal examination with everyone staring. No one took any notice of me or spoke to me. When they'd finished they just left.'

It is hardly surprising that millions of patients are seeking help from 'alternative' practitioners. The truth is that most patients don't desert orthodox doctors because they are looking for better treatments. Most are attracted by alternative medicine because they think it's their only chance of being treated with any respect. And much of the time they're right.

Family doctors (GPs) aren't innocent when it comes to being rude but hospital consultants are by far the worst offenders. Many behave as though they think they are gods. They treat nursing and junior staff like slaves and treat patients with undisguised contempt. Too often hospital consultants act like prison camp guards in Siberia and treat patients as though they are prisoners who've offended the State. Medicine is supposed to be a caring profession but every week thousands of patients make complaints about doctors who have been arrogant, rude and distinctly uncaring.

Here's another letter from a reader:

'When the consultant had finished with me I felt like a piece of meat. As though I was a cow being herded from one place to another. As though I had no feelings and no intellect. I wasn't given the chance to ask any questions. I was so upset that I couldn't get the bus and had to be fetched by a friend. It was a nightmare!'

Doctors often seem to forget that although they may become blasé about death and illness every medical consultation is – to the patient involved – a significant and memorable event.

Many patients complain that hospital consultants show off in front of junior doctors and nurses. (The same doctors are usually said to be polite – even ingratiating – with their private patients). And bad manners are catching – and imitated by nurses, junior doctors and others. I've received thousands of letters from readers complaining about rudeness displayed by nurses, auxiliaries, orderlies, physiotherapists and radiographers. Night nurses seem to annoy more people than any other group. Some hospital staff seem to enjoy humiliating and de-humanising their patients. Pregnant women and the elderly often seem to be treated with least kindness.

Here are more extracts from reader's letters:

Mr A : 'When I told my consultant that I would go mad if I had to put up with my symptoms any longer he said: 'You probably already are, my dear!' He was playing to the gallery and laughing when he said this and his entourage laughed politely to please him.'

Mrs B : 'A consultant showed off to impress younger colleagues. When I murmured a complaint he said: 'No one dragged you in off the streets, did they?'.'

Mrs C: 'A doctor shouted at me because he couldn't get a needle into a vein in my arm.'

Mrs D: 'I went in to see the consultant and he told me I had breast cancer and would need an operation when they could fit me in. That was it. The consultation didn't last more than three minutes. My world had been turned upside down. I went outside, got into my car, drove home in a state of shock and then burst into tears when my children came into the house.'

Mr E: 'When I asked the surgeon who had told me that I needed an operation whether the operation was essential he said: "If you don't want the operation I've got plenty to be getting on with. It makes no difference to me".'

Mrs F: 'When I had a breast X-ray the person who did it was very cruel and rude. My breasts hurt for five days afterwards.'

Mrs G: 'I had to have an intimate examination. A group of doctors gathered around and were laughing and giggling and telling rude jokes. I will never again have an intimate examination. I would rather die.'

Mrs H: 'The consultant asked me if I was feeling better. I said 'No' because I was still in pain. He then shouted at me and I burst into tears. He shouted 'Look at me when I talk to you!' but I couldn't because I was crying so much.'

Mr I: 'My wife has been in hospital three times so far this year but no one has told us anything.'

Mrs J: 'I was so nervous my hands were shaking and I couldn't undo my bra. The doctor shouted at me to hurry up because time was money.'

Mrs K: 'My GP fixed me up with a private appointment with a consultant. It cost me a lot of money. The consultant just said that I needed to see a different sort of specialist and that I should have known. When I didn't pay the bill the consultant's manager phoned up and said I had broken a contract. He has now issued a court summons.'

Mrs L: 'When my husband was in hospital the doctor in charge treated him very badly. Two weeks ago I heard that the doctor had been admitted to the same ward that my husband had been in. I pray to God to forgive me for my thoughts.'

Mrs M: 'I sat on the couch in one of those funny little gowns they give you to wear. Suddenly the screens were pushed aside and a doctor burst in. He ripped open my gown so that I was naked, prodded me about and then left as suddenly as he had arrived. He didn't say a word to me. Ten minutes later a nurse came in to say that I could go.'

Mrs N: 'When I saw the consultant privately he was very nice. But when I had to go and see him in a public clinic he treated me like dirt.'

Mrs O: 'I waited nine months for an appointment at the hospital. But I didn't see a doctor at all. I saw a young student who was very arrogant. I'd have been ashamed of him if he'd been my grandson.'

Mrs P: 'I went into a local hospital for a sterilisation. I was told to arrive before 7.00 am. I was there at 6.30 am. I was totally ignored as were seven or eight other women, all waiting for various operations. At 9.30 am I was told there were no beds but that they would go through with the op and hope that some people were discharged. I was sent to another floor, frightened, alone and stressed to be greeted by some doctor I had never seen before. I was practically thrown onto a trolley and wheeled to theatre with my pre-med tablet being shoved in my hand to swallow on the way. My husband phoned to find out how I was doing and was told he wasn't a real relative (not a blood relative) so no information could be given to him. Afterwards I was left on the trolley with the feeling I was alone and was going to die. I still had the effects of the anaesthetic in my body. The thing used to put the anaesthetic in me was hanging out of my hand. I told them I was allergic to plasters but they still put plasters on my stomach causing a bad, itchy rash. I was left to wander around for a toilet, walking into walls and other trolleys on my own, still only just conscious. I lay on my trolley in a side room no bigger than a cupboard until 4.00 pm with extremely painful backache and no painkillers. A nurse then arrived, gave me a couple of tablets and said they were closing the ward as it was for day patients only. I had to dress myself, phone my husband to pick me up (the right phrase as I could hardly walk) and bring me home. I was told there was no need to return for a check up or any follow up to make sure I was OK. When I went home my pulse rate was 130 a minute. The only thing they gave me was a letter to give my doctor saying I had been sterilised, and a couple of typed lines on a scrap of paper telling me not to drive or drink for 24 hours. How can our health system treat people like this?'

Doctors are supposed to help make people better. But time and time again their thoughtlessness is making people worse.

Doctors often try to excuse their rudeness by complaining that they are overworked. But that is simply not true. In the last 10 years the average doctor's workload has fallen dramatically. According to one report the average family doctor now works a 23 hour week. One doctor boasted that he manages to cram his workload into just seven hours a week.

Hospital consultants are even worse. Many deliberately keep their hospital waiting lists as long as possible so that they'll get more paying patients at their private clinics. Many never even turn up for hospital clinics but instruct junior, untrained doctors to do the work for them. Meanwhile they're busy seeing private patients. Most seem to forget that patients are nervous. They explain nothing and discourage questions. Most regard their time as so important that they instruct administrators to bring patients in hours early. Most forget the fact that patients may be embarrassed at being seen undressed.

Many hospital consultants are beginning to complain about the number of patients who don't turn up for out-patient appointments. Personally, I'm not at all surprised that the number of patients failing to turn up has become an epidemic. I'm more surprised that any patients bother to turn up.

Here are the complaints patients most commonly make to me about hospital consultants and hospital out-patient departments.

1. *'You only get two minutes'*
My investigation shows that this is a slight exaggeration. The average out-patient in some clinics can probably expect to spend three or even four minutes with the doctor. What an insult! What a waste of time.

2. *'The doctor doesn't know anything'*
Most out-patient clinics are run not by consultants but by junior hospital doctors who often have only a few months or even weeks experience. They have probably never seen the patient before. And they'll never see him again.

3. *'No one tells you anything'*
I'm convinced that some hospital doctors are trained by the security services. They never tell patients anything.

#### 4. 'You're treated like dirt'
Too often true. Patients are herded into groups and treated like mentally incompetent aardvarks. Too often nurses give the impression that they got their training at Belsen.

#### 5. 'They keep you waiting for hours'
Oh, boy do they keep patients waiting! You may get less than five minutes with the doctor but it'll take up half a day of your time. Why do hospitals always assume that no one else has anything important to do?

#### 6. 'They don't give you much notice'
A surprising number of patients get less than a week's notice – often after waiting for weeks or months. There is absolutely no excuse for this – apart from incompetence.

#### 7. 'There's no privacy'
Most hospitals seem to assume that patients are exhibitionists. Not true. Most patients dislike having their private parts viewed by orderlies, porters and electricians.

#### 8. 'The doctor doesn't speak my language'
Most patients don't care two hoots where doctors come from as long as they are competent. But all patients like to be treated by doctors who can speak their language.

#### 9. 'They never bother to tell you that an appointment is cancelled'
'I waited five months for an appointment,' complained one patient. 'When I got there I was told that the doctor had gone on holiday a week before and there was no one there who could see me.' Inexcusable. No doctor goes on holiday without giving at least a month's notice. A letter or phone call would save everybody time.

#### 10. 'They only wanted me there for some research project'
Every week thousands of patients waste their time (and money) visiting hospitals where doctors are conducting private research programmes. Many feel 'used'. I don't blame them.

Hospital doctors sometimes do important work. I'm not arguing with that. But there is too much thoughtlessness, too much arrogance and too little thought for the feelings and needs of patients (who are, after all, the people paying everyone's salary).

Frequently, doctors just don't seem to think before they open their mouths.

Just before a trip to Paris I had to have some hospital tests done. After one set of tests a specialist told me that there was a chance that I had cancer. 'But don't worry about it,' he said cheerfully. 'Go and enjoy your stay in Paris. We'll do some more tests when you get back.'

I had to explain that I would find it difficult to relax with such a threat hanging over my head. Within a few hours the extra, additional test had been done and I had been given the 'all clear'. If I hadn't insisted on having my problem sorted out there and then the extra, unnecessary worry could, I suspect, have made me genuinely ill.

Patients would get treated better if doctors always pretended to themselves that every patient they saw was a close relative or loved one.

I've always believed that a doctor should treat every patient as he would want his own family to be treated.

Today's consultants must all hate their families.

Too many doctors seem to believe that they are superior beings; that their authority should never be questioned; that their time is more important than anyone else's and that they are the only people entitled to respect.

I suspect that part of the problem lies in the way that medical students are trained. Although medical students are taught a great deal about disease they are frequently not told very much about patients. They are, I suspect, taught too little about human rights and not enough about a doctor's responsibilities. They are, I fear, also taught too little about the impact a patient's feelings can have on his health.

And part of the problem is the fact that it is too easy for doctors to forget that patients are paying their fat salaries. When no money changes hands in the clinic or consulting room it's too easy for a doctor to forget that the patient is a consumer and is entitled to respect as a right not as a favour. (It would be nice if doctors offered patients respect because they cared about them but that might be too much to hope for).

Certainly when money does change hands doctors seem to be

much nicer. And hospital consultants are more likely to have private patients and two sets of standards.

One reader had first hand experience of this.

To save time she was advised to see a consultant privately, away from the hospital. He was, she says all smiles and charm. He stood up when she entered his consulting room. He was polite, kindly and thoughtful. But the treatment went on for weeks and the bills got bigger and bigger. Eventually my reader couldn't afford any more private treatment. So she made an appointment to see the same consultant in his hospital clinic.

'He was,' she told me, 'rude, insolent and arrogant. He didn't even look up when I went into the consulting room. He examined me but spoke only through the nurse who was with him. He was brusque. No smiles and no handshakes. He seemed a different person.'

What a terrible indictment that is. It isn't just administrators who sometimes give the impression that they would prefer it if their hospitals were empty of patients. A lot of consultants give that impression too.

'Patients are a bloody nuisance,' I'm told an egocentric hospital consultant roared when confronted by a patient who had the audacity to ask a question. 'They clutter up the corridors and bleed all over the wards. We could get twice as much done if they'd all bugger off back home.' His troop of tame, sycophantic, middle-ranking nurses and junior doctors, crowding around him like lakeside ducks waiting for scraps of bread, laughed dutifully.

My informant, the unfortunate patient who had the temerity to question the white coated god, tells me she tried to disappear down the bed and spent the rest of the day shivering with shame, fear and embarrassment.

The tragic truth is that thousands of men and women in white coats are so bad mannered that they would be better suited to work as policemen or debt collectors.

Bad behaviour of this sort isn't just unforgivable bad manners, it's also bad medicine. For years now there has been plenty of evidence to show that patients get better quicker when they are treated kindly. Patients who are given information about their illnesses, and who are treated with courtesy and respect, need fewer drugs and go home quicker than patients who are treated like dirty laundry.

All things considered it is becoming increasingly clear that patients might be better off if hospital doctors – particularly surgeons – were replaced by computers and robots. Indeed, there is now a growing amount of evidence to show that computers practise hospital medicine better than human beings.

♦ One trial has shown that computers are 10 per cent better than consultants at making diagnoses.

♦ A second trial – involving nearly 20,000 patients – confirmed that computers are far better than most doctors at diagnosing patients suffering from severe abdominal pains.

♦ In America, robots have been devised that can assist with hip replacement surgery.

♦ Computer controlled robots are being used to perform brain surgery in France.

♦ Scientists are developing robots that can perform prostate surgery.

♦ In Germany, there are plans to use robots in ear, nose and throat work.

Computers and robots have a number of advantages. They do not get tired. They are speedy and predictable. They are not subject to prejudice. They are far less vulnerable to the blandishments and bribes of the drugs industry. And, of course, they aren't rude, domineering or arrogant. Indeed, they can be programmed to treat patients politely.

I wonder how many patients would prefer a polite, efficient computer to a rude, incompetent human doctor?

* * *

There are two vitally important lessons here.

First, do not let yourself be pushed, bullied, frightened or angered into abandoning orthodox medicine completely. Alternative medicine has its uses and its place but for some illnesses orthodox doctors can provide a more useful, more effective service if they are used properly.

Second, you must learn to stand up for yourself when dealing with doctors. If you don't, then the chances are high that you will be treated without respect. Don't be concerned that by sticking up for yourself you will annoy your doctor and possibly endanger the treatment you receive. All the available evidence shows very clearly that patients who are aggressive and demanding (and, as a result, often unpopular with doctors and nurses), and who ask questions and insist on being told what is happening to them – and why – not only stand a much better chance of getting better but also get better far quicker too.

## 2 │ Tests And Investigations – Are They Safe?

At least two thirds of all the tests and investigations ordered by hospital doctors and family doctors are unnecessary.

♦ One survey has shown that routine blood and urine tests help doctors make a diagnosis in only one per cent of cases.

♦ Another survey showed that when hospital doctors order tests to identify bugs most of the patients involved are sent home before the results of the tests are known.

Unnecessary tests and investigations are ordered for several reasons. Sometimes doctors do them because they feel that they will be less likely to be sued if they can show that they did lots of tests.

And younger doctors may order routine tests so that they'll have all the possible answers available if quizzed by senior consultants.

None of this would matter much if tests were cheap and easy to do and if they were always harmless and reliable. But many of the unnecessary tests doctors order are complex, and expensive.

Even worse many of the investigations which are done result in patients getting the wrong treatment or getting too much treatment and, tragically, tests aren't as reliable as doctors and patients often think they are.

Most laboratory tests are only 95 per cent accurate – even when all the equipment in the laboratory is working absolutely perfectly (something that usually happens about once a week). So if a patient has twenty laboratory tests done then the chances are that even if he is perfectly healthy the tests will show at least one abnormality.

One recent study showed that out of 93 children who had been diagnosed as having heart disease – and who had lived as 'heart patients' – only 17 really had heart disease. The rest had suffered severe restrictions on their activities for no good reason at all.

To all this must be added the fact that many tests are dangerous – and can even kill.

Don't put too much faith in tests. And don't let your doctor perform too many. Tests aren't as necessary, as useful or as reliable as most people think they are.

## 3 | How Will Your Drug Affect You?

Every time your doctor writes out a prescription he is conducting an experiment. He doesn't know exactly what will happen when you take the drug he is prescribing.

One reason for this is the fact that neither pharmaceutical companies nor doctors ever bother to test drugs properly before making them widely available. In an editorial in a leading international journal one commentator admitted that 'only about 15 per cent of medical interventions are supported by solid scientific evidence'. (Yes, you read that correctly: 'only about 15 per cent of medical interventions are supported by solid scientific evidence.')

Another problem is that we are all different. When you take a pill it may give you diarrhoea. When your best friend takes the same drug it may make her constipated. When your uncle takes the same drug it may give him a skin rash. The pill may do its intended job for three, two, one or none of you.

# 4 Is Your Doctor Trying Out A New Drug On You?

Every week thousands of patients are used – often unwittingly – in medical experiments. Doctors in general practice and in hospitals make huge personal bonuses by testing new drugs for pharmaceutical companies. But patients are often put at risk unnecessarily.

Be suspicious if your doctor makes a great fuss of you, is unusually polite or wants you to return to the clinic at very regular intervals. If, instead of handing you a prescription, your doctor gives you a bottle of pills and doesn't charge you for them then the pills may be new and you may be taking part in a drug trial. Watch out if your doctor asks you a lot of questions that don't seem entirely relevant. If your doctor is doing a clinical trial for a drug company he will almost certainly ask you lots of questions about side effects – questions that he would not normally ask. Be wary if your doctor wants you to undergo blood or other tests but doesn't explain why the tests are necessary. Drug companies paying for new drugs to be tested may want blood tests performed.

If your doctor admits that he wants to try out a new drug on you make sure that there is no existing alternative. New drugs should only be tried out on patients when there are no effective and safe alternatives.

Why should you risk your health (and your life) to benefit your doctor's bank balance and the drug company's profits?

## 5 | THE REAL CAUSE OF CANCER – AND THE SOLUTION

The most repressive, prejudiced and obscenely intolerant branch of the international medical industry is undoubtedly that part of it which claims to deal with cancer.

The reason for this is simple: the medical and scientific establishments are largely comprised of men and women whose original thinking (if they ever did any) is long behind them. Cancer is getting commoner but the people in the cancer industry will never find a cure because they're looking in the wrong places. In this chapter I intend to explain why I believe cancer develops – and how you can minimise your chances of developing it.

I should warn you that the medical establishment does not approve of, or agree with, anything that you are about to read. This is, I should also point out, the same medical establishment which doesn't believe that drug side effects are a significant problem, which, for many years denied that benzodiazepine tranquillisers could be addictive, which has ignored the health hazards of meat, fatty food, mobile telephones, X-rays and microwaves and which has sold itself so completely to the drug, chemical and food industries that four out of ten patients who take a drug suffer unpleasant or potentially lethal side effects and that one in six patients in hospital are there because doctors have made them ill. This is the same medical establishment which has for years ignored the relationship between diet and cancer and, indeed, between weight and cancer.

Members of the establishment are committed to supporting long established theories partly because they do not have the breadth of intelligence to cope with anything new, and partly because personal and professional jealousy makes them unwilling to acknowledge any genuinely new and creative ideas which might result in non-establishment scientists acquiring public respect and honour.

This small-town mindset paradigm is made even more repressive by the fact that the cancer industry is now so huge that it requires vast amounts of money simply in order to stay alive.

Since a good deal of that money comes from the drug industry (which is, not surprisingly, only interested in pharmacological solutions) the cancer industry's aims, methods and motives are now indistinguishable from the drug industry's aims, methods and motives.

* * *

In addition to being the most intolerant the modern cancer industry must surely be the least successful branch of medical science ever to have existed.

In my view it is also probably the most corrupt and self-serving. If the cancer industry ever accidentally hit upon a cure for cancer I honestly very much doubt if anyone would hear about it. Finding and publicising a cure for cancer would put the cancer industry employees out of business.

As has been well documented, the incidence of cancer has been, and is, steadily increasing for decades. The cancer industry makes a good deal of noise about the fact that there has been some progress in the treatment of rare forms of cancer in children but the overall death rate from cancer has been increasing steadily for decades. Chemotherapy does not work and has never worked for the cancers which kill nine out of ten cancer patients. One patient described chemotherapy as 'like using a heavy plumber's tool to fix jewellery'. Many patients given chemotherapy and classified as 'cured' go on to develop another cancer within a short period.

The cancer establishment has insisted on sticking with radiotherapy and chemotherapy despite the fact that there is now so much evidence that these approaches do not work that ordinary patients who have no idea that there are alternatives are turning them down; preferring to die quietly and in peace rather than to die of a painful and pointless treatment programme.

The only people who benefit from the modern cancer industry are the people working for the modern cancer industry..

Is it because the drug industry has so much control over the cancer charities (because it gives them money) that the cancer charities seem only interested in research that is likely to uncover drug based cures? (How could a drug company ever make money out of a treatment programme that involved meditation or a change in diet?)

And yet, throughout the world, the modern cancer industry – which steadfastly refuses to acknowledge the fact that 80 per cent of cancers can be prevented or to investigate the many new alternative therapies – is protected by law.

In most western countries it is now actually illegal to offer a treatment for cancer that might work.

Even qualified doctors are only allowed to prescribe chemotherapy or radiotherapy or to send their patients for surgery. The authorities relentlessly persecute those who offer new and possibly effective and non-toxic therapies (ignoring the wishes of patients who wish to try those therapies) while condoning, paying for and protecting by law therapies which are known to be often toxic and frequently ineffective. It is bizarre to see the way that governments tell their citizens that vaccines are all safe, that beef is safe to eat and that chemotherapy is the treatment of choice for cancer. I suspect that governments would tell their citizens that hitting yourself on the head with a hammer was safe if the hammer industry told them to say this. It would be funny were it not so tragic.

Doctors who dare to offer patients new hope and new treatments are scorned, abused, persecuted, vilified, forced to go into hiding or threatened with imprisonment. Honest, well-meaning, caring doctors whose work with cancer patients has won them many followers among the sick, and their relatives, have received nothing but trouble from the authorities.

The problems faced by the proponents of remedies not made by drug companies have been well documented. Anyone who dares to offer an unofficial remedy for cancer is accused of being simply out to make money. This accusation (which is often easy to disprove in the case of doctors and others offering 'alternative' therapies) is, of course, never made about doctors or drug companies, whose work is apparently all done exclusively in the public interest.

The list of doctors who have been persecuted for offering non-orthodox cancer treatments (which invariably seem to work much better than anything offered by the official cancer industry) is as long as the list of alleged cancer 'cures' offered or promised by the cancer industry which have been proven to be of no value, or quietly forgotten once those making the promises had acquired the grants they wanted. In many countries it is illegal for anyone to claim to have a cure for cancer that is not approved by the medical establishment and the pharmaceutical industry. Around the world countless cancer pioneers – including some of the brightest medical brains of the century – have been forced out of business by busybody bureaucrats acting on behalf of the cancer industry. (In one case a policeman who arrested a successful alternative cancer clinic operator consulted the practitioner when his own brother was found to be suffering from terminal cancer. The brother was treated successfully by the practitioner the policeman had persecuted.)

* * *

The medical and scientific establishments have (largely through the fact that they have sold out to the enormously wealthy and powerful international pharmaceutical industry) obtained more or less complete control over politicians and the media. The establishment's unwillingness to rock the boat means that the industry's own paid advocates can pretty much control what ordinary readers get to see. In the UK both the Press Complaints Commission and the Advertising Standards Authority allegedly exist to protect the public. In my experience both organisations are a disgrace and do far more to defend and protect industry than they do to protect the public.

When Britain's Meat and Livestock Commission complained about a column of mine which reported that meat causes cancer the Press Complaints Commission rolled over like a playful puppy and was quick to defend the interests of the meat industry by ignoring the evidence and finding in favour of the meat industry and against me. I had supplied scientific evidence in support of my arguments but the PCC didn't seem too impressed with independent scientific research work when put against the views of those defending the meat industry. I wasn't allowed to appeal against this bizarre judgement.

Britain's Advertising Standards Authority (ASA) is no better. Advertisements for my book *Food for Thought* were banned by the ASA because I had dared to include, in the book, advice on what sort of diet to eat in order to reduce the chance of developing cancer. I listed the foods that are known to cause cancer and the foods which are known to provide some protection.

The ASA claims to exist to protect the public but I find it difficult to see how banning advertisements for a book that contains a summary of scientifically based clinical advice on how to avoid cancer can possibly protect the public. It seems to me that, wittingly or unwittingly, the ASA was simply protecting the cancer establishment and helping to ensure that the number of people developing cancer continues to increase. There is more about both the PCC and the ASA in my book *Fighting For Animals*.

In my view Britain would be a safer place for people (though a less profitable one for cancer producing industries) if the PCC and the ASA were quietly disbanded. I suspect that much the same is true for similar organisations in other countries.

* * *

There are now many alternative therapies available for the treatment of cancer. Some are available very cheaply. Some are extremely expensive. Some are simple to follow. Some are extremely complex.

But the two things that the successful anti-cancer therapies all have in common (and the multi-billion-dollar a year cancer industry either hasn't realised this yet or else refuses to act on it) is that, whether they are designed to do this or not, the so-called alternative therapies which work, and which often have extraordinary and dramatic results when applied to seriously ill cancer patients, all improve the health and vitality of the body's immune system and help eradicate chemical toxins from the body.

The alternative cancer therapies which work offer diets which are rich in vitamin packed organic fruit and vegetables and low in toxic chemicals, and encourage patients to learn how to relax and to find some peace in their lives. It doesn't matter whether the peace comes through meditation, relaxation, religion or love and comfort applied by people who care.

Despite all the billions of dollars spent on research no one yet knows how cancer develops. One theory is that free radicals – molecules produced routinely within the body – may damage the DNA within our cells, transforming a previously normal cell into a potentially cancerous cell. Every cell in the human body needs oxygen but oxygen is responsible for the production of free radicals – oxygen carrying molecules which are destructive and aggressive. It is free radicals which encourage our tissues and bodies to age and which cause damage to cells and tissues when our immune systems falter. The formation of free radicals is an inevitable part of life. (And is added to by pollutants from the outside world. For example, a smoker breathes in several billion free radicals every time he sucks on a cigarette.)

Fortunately, it is now believed that there are some food substances called antioxidants which can neutralise free radicals which are formed. There are four known antioxidants at the moment: beta-carotene (which is converted in the human body to vitamin A), vitamins C and E and the mineral selenium. There is a growing amount of evidence to show that antioxidants can help reduce the likelihood of numerous diseases including: cancer, arteriosclerosis, heart disease, skin diseases, types of arthritis, Parkinson's disease, cataracts, Alzheimer's disease and radiation damage.

A good diet and plenty of relaxation are the stable, ever present qualities of the effective anti-cancer cures which work.

\* \* \*

If you measure the cancer industry by the money it brings in, it is one of the most successful industries in the world.

If you measure the cancer industry by its success in defeating the disease and saving patients it is one of the most unsuccessful and fraudulent industries in the world.

During the last few years over $200,000,000,000 has been spent on cancer research. That's a lot of noughts.

The cancer industry's success or failure in helping to combat cancer is easy to measure.

Every figure examined shows that the so-called 'War against Cancer' is, and always has been, a sham. Whether we look at the number of people getting cancer, or the number of people surviving when they do get it, the figures show that the cancer charities, the drug companies, the taxpayer funded laboratories and the rest of the cancer industry have failed miserably, are failing miserably and will almost certainly continue to fail miserably.

Look, first, at the way that the number of people getting cancer has increased:

♦ In 1971 one in six people were likely to develop cancer.

♦ Ten years later, by 1981, the risk had doubled and one in three people were likely to develop cancer at some stage in their lives.

♦ By the late 1990s the figures had worsened still further: with 41 per cent of men and 38 per cent of women likely to develop cancer at least once.

Not much of an advertisement for the cancer industry so far.

But what about the survival rates for cancer?

Well, after billions of dollars and decades of research the survival rates are exactly the same today – 2001 – as they were in 1950.

The cancer industry gets its most significant statistics by looking at how many people live for five years after their cancer was first diagnosed.

Half a century ago the five year survival rate for patients who developed cancer was around one in three.

And that is what it is today – around one in three.

In fact the real figures are even worse than these.

The tens of thousands working in the cancer industry are so desperate to disguise the truth of their appalling failure that they have fiddled the figures. By comparing today's figures with the figures from thirty, forty or fifty years ago they are not comparing 'like' with 'like'.

They have done this by encouraging doctors (and patients) to diagnose cancer earlier and earlier. Having an earlier diagnosis made probably doesn't make much (if any) difference to the length of time the patient will live but it does mean that people join the statistics at an earlier point in their illness.

Bizarrely, the cancer industry regards a patient who has survived for five years as having been cured (though only if he or she has been treated by orthodox methods). Even if that patient dies after five years and one minute he or she will be counted as an official success. Clearly the earlier the diagnosis is made the better the figures will look. Imagine just how bad the figures would be without this massage.

As far as the cancer industry is concerned the sole aim of treatment is to keep a patient alive for that magical five years. I worry that they don't care if the treatment kills the patient later (as chemotherapy and radiotherapy are likely to do).

They have also fiddled the figures by changing the diagnostic rules to make their own figures look better. By widening the net and including as 'cancer' patients many who would not have previously been officially regarded as having cancer they can improve their figures still further.

(The medical establishment seems to do this regularly. The massive and enormously profitable AIDS industry has changed its own rules so that patients dying from tuberculosis, for example, are now included in the statistics for AIDS patients.)

The conclusion has to be that the cancer industry – the big cancer charities, government sponsored research laboratories and drug companies – have been wasting time, energy, manpower and money. There is no evidence that catching cancer symptoms early increases survival. Most surveys suggest that untreated cancer patients may survive for longer than patients who have orthodox treatment. One famous study showed that patients who refused orthodox 'cancer industry' treatment (from the limited 'slash, poison or burn' regimes) lived for an average of 12.5 years while those patients who accepted 'cancer industry' treatment lived, on average for just three years. Patients who have radiation, chemotherapy or surgery often feel worse too.

\* \* \*

Cancer treatment is a huge money spinner for drug companies and charities. The cancer industry uses clever (dishonest) advertising to pull in donations and legacies. Cancer charities bring in a fortune through their high street charity shops. The cancer industry creates endless myths about forthcoming cancer cures, vaccines to prevent cancer, drugs to cure it. 'Give us a pound,' they say, 'and you don't have to worry about cancer. If you give us a pound you can carry on eating burgers and smoking cigarettes.' And so, inevitably, people give them a pound (or more) and carry on eating burgers and smoking cigarettes.

For patients – and healthy citizens – the 'war on cancer' is, and always has been, an abject failure; constantly using fake promises and false hopes to help increase profits.

Can there have ever been a more dishonest, more disreputable, more cynical or more immoral industry?

(At least the tobacco industry has never claimed to be *looking* for a cure for cancer.)

The vast majority of those involved in the cancer industry are dishonest; biased, bought and too scared of their industry paymasters to acknowledge the truth. The remainder are simply stupid.

Carcinogenic chemicals and technologies are assumed innocent until proved guilty (and no one puts much effort into trying to prove anything guilty when there are profits to be considered), hardly any truly independent research is ever done and when research is done it usually involves animals.

(The researchers should know that research work on animals is entirely useless and irrelevant but they do it because it buys time for their industry paymasters.)

\* \* \*

The people working in the cancer industry will claim that they are winning the battle. They are lying. The incidence of cancer has been steadily increasing for decades. There has been a fifty per cent increase in the incidence of cancer since America's 'War Against Cancer' was launched thirty years ago.

Around 90 per cent of the money given to cancer research is spent on searching for and testing expensive (and immensely profitable) high tech cures. (Chemotherapy – possibly the most harmful, useless form of treatment yet devised by man – can cost in excess of £100,000 per year, per patient, with the vast majority of that sum being pure profit.)

And, of course, some 'fashionable' cancers receive far more than their fair share of attention from cancer researchers.

I've been screaming about this for a quarter of a century (since the publication of my second book *Paper Doctors* in 1976), so it was something of a relief to see the UK Government accept in 2003 that cancer research money isn't allocated either fairly or logically.

Around £500,000,000 a year is spent on cancer research in the UK alone. Most of that money comes from donors to charity and from taxpayers. But, partly through pressure from politically correct politicians and partly because cancer charities know that some varieties of cancer are more 'fashionable' and publicly acceptable than others, the allocation of all this money is downright unfair.

Vast amounts of research money is spent on studying breast cancer, cervical cancer and leukaemia, for example, but relatively little is spent investigating bowel cancer, prostate cancer or lung cancer.

Of course, the real tragedy is that most of the money is wasted anyway because researchers aren't innovative, aren't imaginative and aren't particularly well-informed about the best ways to research, prevent or treat the disease. Despite all the expenditure of so much money the incidence of cancer continues to rise. The 'war' against cancer has been just as much of a failure as the 'war' against drugs.

Indeed, the evidence shows that the global cancer establishment – consisting of government departments, charities and drug companies – has, largely for commercial reasons, successfully suppressed a number of possible cancer 'cures'.

And very little money or effort is put into cancer prevention. Most people, for example, are still totally unaware of the well-established links between diet and cancer.

Not surprisingly, the cancer industry rarely investigates the responsibility of the chemical industries in the increasing incidence of cancer. This may, of course, be because the chemical industries make many of the products used to treat the cancers their industries have caused.

* * *

In the cancer industry, as within other areas of the medical establishment, the hugely influential, and theoretically independent, intellectual and academic infrastructure has been corrupted by inducements that would in other societies simply be known as 'bribes' but which in our society are known as grants, bursaries, honoraria, consultancies, directorships, share options, expense accounts and so on.

At the same time allegedly independent experts are bribed by the government with powerful positions on advisory and regulatory bodies. These positions do not need to be highly paid. The people who accept these posts know that their status will entitle them to claim more grants, bursaries, honoraria, consultancies, directorships, share options, expense accounts and so on.

There are very few influential people in medicine, food technology, genetic engineering, life sciences and biotechnology who have not been bought by the powerful industry/government combination.

The result is that those who oppose the new establishment are easy to discredit and denounce. They can be quickly destroyed professionally and personally. The media is controlled and bought, often by politicians doing deals (encourage your readers to vote for us and we will keep the Monopolies Commission off your back when you want to buy another TV station). Specialist health and science correspondents are usually so ignorant that they are totally dependent upon what they are told by the establishment experts. They are frightened of losing their jobs and always willing to buy promotion (and lucrative outside assignments writing for drug company publications) by 'monstering' anyone who dares to disagree with the establishment line.

It is hardly surprising that cancer is becoming commoner by the year. And hardly surprising that survival rates are so poor.

Just how people working for the big professional cancer organisations can sleep at night I cannot imagine. Personally, I have absolutely no doubt that if the big cancer charities had never existed there would be far, far fewer people dying from cancer in the world today. Without such groups genuinely effective alternative approaches to cancer prevention and treatment would have stood a far greater chance of reaching a wide audience.

\* \* \*

Why has the cancer industry failed so miserably to reduce the number of people developing cancer and failed, equally miserably, to improve the survival rates of those who get it?

There are several explanations.

1. The profit, the cancer industry knows well, is in looking for a cure rather than actually finding one. I suspect that the scientists who work for the big cancer charities would run a mile in the opposite direction if they thought they had accidentally stumbled on a cure for cancer. If the big cancer charities did find a cure for cancer all the scientists, bureaucrats, publicists and marketing experts who work for these charities would have to find other (probably less lucrative) employment.

This explanation may seem unlikely – even paranoid or conspiratorial – but it does offer one explanation for the fact that the cancer industry insists that only orthodox medicine can offer a cure for cancer. And the cancer industry is so powerful that it has influenced governments in its favour. Bizarrely, in most countries of the world it is now illegal to offer an alternative cancer treatment (even if it works). Doctors who dare to recommend, or even discuss, alternative therapies are isolated, reviled, belittled and ridiculed. The establishment is not above watching individuals who are deemed to be a threat. Premises may be entered and phones tapped. Advisory bodies who decide who is to be excommunicated or punished are often populated by experts who are paid by the companies they are supposed to be supervising. The cancer industry is self-preserving. It encourages its members to deny and discourage remedies which may turn out to be real cures.

When a popular newspaper reported that a 27-year-old woman had 'shunned life-saving drugs' and it was suggested that her success might be due to the fact that she had eaten over six tons of fruit and vegetables during a two year battle with cancer a spokesman for the a cancer charity was reported to have said: 'I'm convinced it was conventional treatment which pushed the cancer into remission. She took a big risk in abandoning chemotherapy and we don't advise others to do the same.'

Since the woman had taken just one dose of chemotherapy this is a bizarre claim. The cancer charity did not seem interested in investigating the miracle cure – let alone finding out whether it might provide hope for other patients. Their main interest was, it seems to me, to defend the financial interests of the medical profession and the pharmaceutical industry. The official credit for any patient's recovery will always be given to drugs or to a single consultation with an orthodox physician rather than to any alternative therapy.

2. The cancer charities are inextricably linked to the big pharmaceutical industries. Naturally, the big drug companies aren't terribly interested in cures which don't involve drugs. They tolerate surgery because it keeps the members of the medical profession happy and because patients who have surgery are usually given chemotherapy as well. They accept radiotherapy partly because the companies making and selling radiotherapy equipment are part of the cancer industry and partly because patients who have radiotherapy usually have chemotherapy too.

When the hugely wealthy cancer industry did get involved with a trial of a popular type of alternative medicine the trial was so full of errors that it was worthless. Nevertheless the charity involved held a press conference and made sure that the faulty research (which naturally questioned the value of the alternative approach) got massive national publicity. The alternative approach to the treatment of cancer was vilified as at best worthless and at worst dangerous. Only much later was it made clear that the research which had been done was so flawed as to be useless. One of the scientists involved subsequently cut his throat and killed himself (one assumes that he did so through shame). Before doing so he admitted 'The study was not as good as it could have been.'

Nevertheless, despite the cruel dishonesty of the cancer industry it was the alternative form of treatment which was pretty well destroyed. The established controlled media concentrated on the results of the invalid research and gave little space to the subsequent revelation that the results were worthless.

This is nothing particularly unusual in the world of medicine. The results of medical research often depend upon who is paying.

3. Even after all these years the people who work for the cancer industry still don't seem to understand the relationship between cancer and the body's immune system.

I believe that cancer develops because the body is a wreck.

Because of the accumulated stresses the immune system doesn't work properly and so the toxic chemicals and other irritants which have collected in the body trigger off the development of a cancer.

When I launched a free website to teach internet users the value of a healthy immune system a cancer charity was not amused.

You might imagine that as an organisation ostensibly existing to fight cancer they would have been delighted. Not a bit of it.

'Celeb doctor Vernon Coleman's latest web venture has been branded 'scary, frightening and wrong' by the Cancer Research Campaign,' claimed *The Daily Mirror*, a British newspaper. 'But his views on cancer take a more sinister turn. He claims the medical industry is sacrificing the lives of thousands of cancer sufferers by offering ineffective treatments simply to line the pockets of drug companies.'

'The CRC believes that this is seriously dangerous,' continued *The Daily Mirror*. 'It's awful to think of someone who has just been diagnosed with cancer reading this. The information is wrong. The whole thing is frightening,' said a spokesperson.'

None of the information on my website was wrong, of course. And, it seemed to me, that by its response The Cancer Research Campaign proved that my accusations about the cancer industry were absolutely accurate. (Sadly, that website no longer exists. The site was destroyed by hackers.)

Cancer develops because the body's immune system isn't working well and it is the breakdown of the body's immune system which leads to death. The fitter and stronger the immune system is the less likely a patient will be to develop cancer and the less likely he or she will be to succumb to cancer if he or she develops it. The orthodox doctor, working under the guidelines of the cancer industry views the symptoms of the cancer as the problem. In my view, this is nonsense.

The official view is that if you attack the cancer with surgery, poison or radiotherapy the disease will be eradicated. No one seems interested in why the patient has developed cancer. (Not being interested in the basic cause is a modern malaise. Politicians seem quite disinterested in the causes of terrorism or crime. Doctors don't seem to care a jot about why people develop heart disease or stress related problems.)

No one within the cancer industry is interested in building up the patient's general health or immune system. No one in the cancer industry seems to realise that the official forms of treatment attack and weaken the body (and the immune system) as much as they attack and weaken the cancer. The cancer industry (targeting profit rather than cure) prefers to turn every patient into a bald, hopeless, eczematous invalid rather than face this simple truth.

4. The cancer industry spends a pittance on teaching people how to avoid cancer. I know what causes eight out of ten cancers. I can tell you the names of the foods, the drinks, the drugs that cause cancer. And the cancer industry can tell you that too. But they don't spend enough money or effort on prevention. The only possible conclusion is that they don't want to cut the incidence of cancer because if they do people will be less afraid of the disease and the cancer industry's income (and profits) will go down. The cancer industry thrives on fear and ignorance. Prevention is not something into which they put a lot of effort – though they are enthusiastic about interventionist techniques for diagnosing cancer as early as possible. For example, women who are susceptible to breast cancer are encouraged to have their breasts X-rayed. This is dangerous. Mammography is one of the most remarkably stupid things ever done in medicine. Can you think of anything dafter than assessing a part of the body known to be exceptionally sensitive to cancer with a diagnostic technique known to cause cancer? Mammography is a profitable business. Plenty of work for doctors and the companies making the mammography machines. And there are three bonuses for the cancer industry. The first is that mammography programmes encourage more fear about cancer. That's good for the cancer industry. It pulls in the money. The second is that by diagnosing patients earlier more of them will survive for five years. (This will make the cancer industry look good because they will be

able to claim that five year survival rates are improving.) And the third is that when women are diagnosed as having early breast cancer they will probably be given the drug tamoxifen to take. Lots more profits there. (The additional, extra bonus is the fact that worry and fear about breast cancer mean that there is now tremendous pressure on doctors to prescribe the drug tamoxifen to healthy women. Tamoxifen is known to cause cancer of the uterus but the drug companies claim that it will help prevent breast cancer. If they have their way just about every woman over the age of 16 will soon be regularly taking this drug.)

Patients are not, however, told to avoid eating meat – even though there is a clear link between meat consumption and breast cancer.

(It is crucial to remember that diagnosing cancer early is 'good' for the cancer industry because it helps to improve five year survival rates. Helping people to *avoid* cancer doesn't help the cancer industry at all.)

5. The crucial fact that the cancer industry overlooks is that our bodies are remarkably capable of looking after themselves.

Few people take advantage of these self-healing mechanisms and protective capabilities because we are all encouraged to put our health and our lives into the hands of the so-called experts – practitioners who are often trained to look at our bodies and the diseases which afflict them with all the breadth of vision of a man looking through the wrong end of a telescope.

The great tragedy of orthodox medicine is that doctors have always been suspicious of anything new and often reluctant to listen to theories and ideas which contradict traditional attitudes.

From Paracelsus to Lind to Semmelweiss, medical history is littered with doctors who learned the hard way that the medical establishment does not take kindly to original ideas or to new concepts which threaten the status quo.

Medical students are taught that they should avoid asking uncomfortable questions and young doctors who wish to succeed know that they must remain unquestioningly faithful to the established truths.

Any physician who rocks the boat, makes waves or swims against the tide will soon find himself floundering in deep water – and struggling to survive.

To be successful in our society a physician must respect the prejudices of his elders, adhere to the dogma of his teachers and shut his mind to theories which do not fit in with orthodox medical doctrines.

Modern medicine is, much like the black magic medicine of the middle ages, an unstructured, unscientific discipline in which uncertainty, confusion and ignorance are too often disguised with conceit, arrogance and bigotry.

At a time when the half-life of medical information is shrinking and the limits of traditional, interventionist medicine are daily becoming more and more apparent, this ostrich-type behaviour is difficult to understand and impossible to justify.

Unless doctors are prepared to consider the unexpected, the unlikely and even the apparently impossible, patients must regard rigidly orthodox interventionists with a certain amount of suspicion and cynicism.

The fact is that our bodies have far more power than we give them credit for.

In the early 1980s I wrote a book called *Bodypower* in which I observed that the body's self-healing mechanisms are so effective that in nine out of ten illnesses the body will deal with any outside disorder itself – without any outside intervention.

If you look after your body well you will dramatically reduce your chances of developing heart disease, cancer or any other threat to your survival.

Moreover, if you do fall ill then you can help yourself recover by taking advantage of those internal self-healing powers and, if necessary, by helping your bodypower.

When a disease threatens the very survival of the organism then the body needs to be encouraged to use all its internal healing powers in order to alter the circumstances within. You need to turn up the boost on your bodypower.

When the circumstances change then the cancer won't grow. When the body is stronger than the cancer the cancer will be defeated. And that, surely, is the key to success in defeating cancer: not to try to destroy the cancer from the outside but to try to help the body defeat the cancer from the inside.

One of the fundamental errors doctors make is that they assume that they can treat cancer (and other life-threatening diseases) in the same way that they thought they could treat infectious diseases.

Tackling cancer as though it were an outside agent (such as a virus or a bacterium) simply doesn't work because cancer is not something that comes in from the outside of the body – it is something that develops within as a result of a fundamental problem inside the human body.

But there *is* a vital lesson to be learnt from the way that our bodies respond to infectious diseases.

Doctors have observed that when patients fall ill with an infectious disease they are more likely to go into spontaneous remission.

Well over a century ago a Frenchman called Dr Didot noted that if prostitutes had syphilis they were very unlikely to develop cancer. Didot actually treated 20 cancer patients with syphilis and 14 of the 20 went into total remission. (I rather doubt if the authorities – which happily approve of toxic chemotherapy – would allow anyone to perform any such experiment today.)

Similarly, whereas cancer is uncommon in areas where malaria is present getting rid of the malaria in an area will result in a rise in the cancer rate.

It has also been reported that people who *have* cancer and who catch malaria have a good chance of going into remission.

Now why could this be?

I have seen it argued that the infectious disease somehow eats up the cancer.

But I don't think that this is what happens at all.

What I believe happens is that patients with cancer who develop an infection get better because their immune systems are triggered into a response. The infection is easily recognised as an immediate threat to the body (in contrast to a cancer which may not be such an immediate and obvious threat) and so the body reacts in the only way it knows how – by winding up the immune system; the result is that the bodypower effect comes into operation and the cancer gets defeated along with the infection.

6. The methods favoured by the cancer industry are, inevitably perhaps, the methods favoured by the medical establishment and the pharmaceutical industry: chemotherapy, surgery and radiotherapy.

Chemotherapy works by poisoning cancer cells. If the drugs only poisoned the cancer cells this would be wonderful. But the problem is that normal cells also die. Chemotherapy drugs are so toxic that they kill just about everything they reach. The prescribing doctor has to carefully adjust the dose of the drug he is prescribing so as to kill the cancer cells without killing too many of the body's essential cells. This is by no means an exact science. Indeed, it isn't really a science at all. It's guesswork and hope. The concept of chemotherapy pays no attention at all to the body's in-built defence mechanisms. On the contrary chemotherapy reduces the effectiveness of the body's defence system and therefore makes it easier for a cancer to grow. Virtually all chemotherapy drugs are immunosuppressive (thereby destroying the body's self-defence mechanisms) and carcinogenic (subsequently producing additional, new cancers). Possible side effects known to be associated with chemotherapy may include: nausea, vomiting, bleeding, loss of hair, liver damage, kidney damage, increased risk of infection, impotence, sterility, bone marrow damage, nerve damage, lung damage, diarrhoea, skin sores, mouth sores, heart damage, allergies and fever. And, of course, an increased susceptibility to another type of cancer. Drugs mask problems rather than deal with them directly. They do not deal with the disease process. They are unnatural. They contaminate the patient and produce an array of confusing side effects. They cover up symptoms which might be of use in leading the doctor to a better form of treatment. Only an intellectually disadvantaged brick would argue that chemotherapy is the way forward for cancer therapy. It is worrying that thousands of people employed in the cancer industry seem to be either intellectually disadvantaged bricks or else in the pay of the pharmaceutical giants. Maybe this is why the so-called war on cancer has been such a complete failure.

There is little or no evidence that radiotherapy works. But plenty of evidence that it can do harm. Most of the available evidence seems to suggest that while the upside is slight the downside is considerable. With radiation there is a powerful risk that the patient will be seriously damaged and disabled. When one reader was advised to have radiotherapy treatment she wisely asked the consultant recommending the therapy to let her see medical evidence supporting the advice. The consultant sent along two scientific papers. One of the papers did not relate to patients in her age group. The other proved that for patients with her particular clinical problem radiotherapy was worse than useless. Hardly reassuring.

* * *

The war against cancer will continue to fail. Avoidable cancers will continue to become commoner and commoner and the establishment will continue to ensure that only the toxic (but highly profitable) alleged treatments of cancer which are authorised by the pharmaceutical industry will be authorised by governments.

Our food, our homes and our general environment are all irretrievably polluted by chemicals. And the pollution is getting worse daily. New chemicals are being created, introduced and sold far faster than anyone can be expected to keep up with them.

Chemicals are, without a doubt, a major cause of death and illness today. They are one of the main reasons why the incidence of cancer continues to rise. The use of untested chemicals is one of the main reasons why the number of babies born with deformities is constantly going up.

Look in your kitchen cupboards, take a look at some of the labels on the foods you've bought, or the cleaning or bathroom products you've got, and you'll see the names of just a fraction of the vast number of chemicals now used as dyes, flavourings, preservatives, disinfectants and so on.

Many of these chemicals are known to be carcinogenic – and yet manufacturers are allowed to continue to use them in a wide variety of products. Thousands have not yet been tested – and we know next to nothing about them. Every day we touch, breathe in and swallow chemicals about which no one knows very much at all. It hardly seems believable. But it's true.

Some of these chemicals produce skin rashes, headaches, irritated eyes, hair damage and other annoying but hardly life-threatening symptoms. Some cause nausea, vomiting and diarrhoea. Others can cause liver or kidney damage, cancer and death. Your local supermarket sells enough dangerous chemicals for you to start a biological war in your neighbourhood.

The companies which make and use these chemicals are trusted to do their own safety tests. New chemicals are used if the company making them decides that they are safe. There are tens of thousands of chemicals around about which the so-called regulatory authorities know no more than you or I know.

Companies which use chemicals do so because they help them increase profits. That's what these companies exist for: to make profits.

There is absolutely nothing wrong with that, of course. But it is something that governments and regulatory authorities seem to forget.

If a company discovers that one of the products it uses may cause cancer is it really likely to announce this to the world – and risk finding itself the subject of a mass of lawsuits? Or is it more likely either to suppress the evidence and continue to use the chemical, or to quietly remove the chemical and replace it with something else?

Chemicals which affect the normal action of hormones in the body (known as endocrine disrupters) have been a special worry for some time. Under normal circumstances the human endocrine system is constantly producing hormones which send signals around the body, switching functions on and off and generally regulating the way the body operates.

Hormones do their job by fitting into special receptors. When the right hormone slips into the right receptor the response is rather like putting a key into a lock: the body responds by doing whatever is appropriate.

Chemicals – found in the food we eat, the air we breathe, the water we drink and the chemicals we use to clean our homes – can interfere with this process by fitting into the receptors and either opening the lock or blocking it so that it cannot open even when the proper hormone arrives. Either way, chaos can ensue.

* * *

Cancer charities and governments aren't the only ones responsible for the remorseless rise in the incidence of cancer. Drug companies must take much of the blame too.

For decades pharmaceutical companies have been members of by far the most profitable industry in the world.

The production and sale of prescription medicines has been a cartel for many years and the big drug companies have carved up and controlled the sale of medicines throughout the world. Companies and individuals who have tried to prepare and offer for sale drugs (or other products) which they believe might be efficacious have been blocked by numerous government agencies – all ostensibly protecting the public but, in practice, defending the profitability of the big drug companies.

Imagine, for example, that you had discovered a herbal recipe which cured cancer. You might want to sell – or even give away – your product so as to reduce the incidence of cancer in the world. No chance. You would be stopped dead in your tracks. In the USA the drug companies are defended by an agency whose agents carry guns and wear gas masks and flak jackets.

The government agencies which are supposed to regulate industries and protect the public now protect industries and regulate the public. Even the mass media cooperate with this policy. Next time you see, hear or read a programme or article about cancer look carefully. You will almost certainly see that the pronouncements made by employees of the official, orthodox cancer industry are treated as though they were written in stone and handed down from on high whereas comments made by those endeavouring to outline the disadvantages of orthodox therapy and the advantages of alternative therapies will be presented with doubt, scepticism and, possibly, derision.

Information provided by the cancer industry is invariably offered up as 'fact' whereas information provided by those advocating alternative approaches will be presented with an indigestible concoction of 'alleges' and 'in their opinions'.

Innovations are quickly and effectively suppressed by governments in case they prove to be a financial threat to the cartel.

Try to sell – or even give away – a cure for cancer (however genuine and however honourable your motives) and you'll be raided. You will end up in prison – with your assets confiscated. If that wasn't enough to put you off try this: to get your new product approved for sale will cost you around $250 million – and you may have to wait a decade before you can sell the product and bring in any money to pay off your debts.

The big drug companies happily put up with these absurd costs because they provide them with protection against competitors.

The big drug companies have it made. They make vast profits from selling legal drugs. (I have described in numerous books the obscene profits which can be made from the sale of prescription drugs – and the ways in which drug companies ensure that their profits remain high.) The only competition they face comes from other, existing, big drug companies.

Any newcomer is forbidden by law from advertising their product until they have official approval – at a cost of a quarter of a billion dollars.

The drug companies protect themselves by claiming that all this is done to protect the public from unscrupulous people trying to sell unsafe, ineffective and extremely expensive products.

Er. Excuse me. Isn't that exactly what the drug industry does?

Brilliant, independent doctors and scientists are specifically forbidden from breaking into the business of selling drugs.

There is no place for entrepreneurs in the cancer industry – or, indeed, in any branch of medicine.

Governments and drug companies control doctors and they control the production and sale of drugs.

In recent years drug companies have become increasingly irritated by small, rival companies selling herbal remedies and supplements. These products have been popular among patients who have been disillusioned by the drug industry and its dangerous, ineffective medicines. The companies selling supplements have sidestepped the cartel because their products have not officially been classified as medicines. But the drug companies have now clamped down and put an end to this and have forced governments around the world (including, the EU, of course) to close down those selling these 'unofficial' medicines. The only crooks officially allowed in the world of medicine are the crooks who have for decades been promoting, selling and making huge profits out of dangerous and ineffective prescription medicines.

Patients everywhere would be better off if small companies were allowed to set up and sell drugs. There would be new ideas, it would be possible to test herbal products which are rumoured to cure cancer (and other serious disorders) and the drug industry would be broken apart and replaced with people with talent and, perhaps, a little honour.

There are plenty of existing laws suitable for protecting patients against crooks and charlatans.

Breaking up the international drug industry would mean that the biggest crooks and charlatans would be out of business.

## 6 Are You Taking Too Many Antibiotics?

When antibiotics – drugs such as penicillin – were first introduced in the 1930s they gave doctors a chance to kill the bacteria causing infections and to save the lives of patients who would otherwise have died of infections such as pneumonia. Antibiotics were regarded as genuine life-savers; heralding a revolution in health care.

Although it is certainly true that the impact made by antibiotics has been exaggerated (many of the diseases which are caused by organisms which are susceptible to antibiotics were on the decline before the antibiotics were introduced) these drugs are undoubtedly of considerable value.

The problem is that although doctors are aware of the advantages of these drugs (if they are in any doubt the drug companies will frequently remind them) they seem unaware of the hazards associated with their unnecessary use.

If you have a serious or troublesome infection – bronchitis, sore throat or cystitis for example – the chances are high that your doctor will prescribe an antibiotic.

If you are innocent and naive you might imagine that the prescribing of an antibiotic will have been done scientifically and that your doctor, as a man or woman of science, will have carefully chosen a drug specifically designed to eradicate the type of bug causing your infection and prescribed for precisely the right number of days.

You would, however, be quite wrong to assume that doctors know what they are doing when they prescribe antibiotics. Antibiotics are powerful drugs. They do save lives. But, in general, they are prescribed with neither sound logic nor scientific understanding. The prescribing of antibiotics is a virtually random exercise. The average tapioca brained traffic warden could prescribe them with as much sense and understanding as the average doctor. Visit one doctor with cystitis and she will give you enough antibiotics to last you for five days. Visit the doctor next door, complaining of exactly the same symptoms, and he may prescribe the same antibiotic but give you enough pills to last for seven days. And visit a third doctor and she may give you pills to last for ten or even fourteen days. Where, in the name of Areolus Phillipus Theophrastus Bombastus von Hohenheim, is the sense in any of this?

This bizarre situation occurs not because doctors haven't bothered to learn how to prescribe antibiotics but because no one knows how antibiotics should be prescribed. Astonishingly, no tests have ever been done to find out precisely for how long antibiotics should be given. Research scientists have been far too busy enjoying themselves doing unspeakable things to monkeys, cats and puppies to bother doing such useful or practical research.

All that is bad enough. But it isn't the end of the horror story. For although scientists know which antibiotics should be used to combat which bugs, the evidence shows that the selection of a drug to prescribe is generally done with the sort of scientific judgement the average six-year-old might apply when picking a coloured sweet out of a box.

As any regular surgery goer will know, there are scores of antibiotics available. Some of these pills are simply variations on profitable themes. But there are some important differences between many of these pills. Drugs are designed to combat specific types of infection. However, most doctors don't usually bother to try to match antibiotics with bugs; instead they simply write out a prescription for any old drug. They tend to choose a drug because they like the name – or can spell it – rather than because it is appropriate.

The end result is that although you might think that the antibiotic you are prescribed has been chosen specifically for your infection you would probably be wrong. Your doctor will have probably simply picked a name at random. She is more likely to prescribe a drug because its name appears on the free disposable pen she happens to be holding than because she knows that it is the best and most suitable drug to kill the bug with which you are infected. Worse still, most doctors are so darned stupid that they happily prescribe antibiotics for virus infections even though viruses are not susceptible to antibiotic therapy.

Today, one in six of the prescriptions doctors write is for an antibiotic and there are at least 100 preparations available for doctors to choose from. Sadly, there is no doubt that most of the prescriptions which are written for antibiotics are unnecessary. Many patients are suffering from viral infections which are not susceptible to antibiotics, and others would get better by themselves without any drug being prescribed. Various independent experts who have studied the use of antibiotics claim that between 50 – 90 per cent of the prescriptions written for antibiotics are unnecessary.

To a certain extent doctors overprescribe because they like to do something when faced with a patient – and prescribing a drug is virtually the only thing most of them can do. To some extent prescribing a drug is a defence against any possible future charge of negligence (on the basis that if the patient dies it is better to have done something than to have done nothing).

But the main reason for the overprescribing of antibiotics is, without doubt, the fact that too many doctors are under the influence of the drug companies.

The overprescribing of antibiotics would not matter too much if these drugs were harmless, and if there were no other hazards associated with their use. But antibiotics are certainly not harmless. I believe that antibiotics kill thousands of patients a year and if nine out of ten prescriptions for antibiotics are unnecessary then it is not unreasonable to assume that nine out of ten of those deaths are unnecessary too.

And antibiotics don't only kill patients. The unnecessary and excessive use of antibiotics causes allergy reactions, side effects and a huge variety of serious complications.

There is also the very real hazard that by overusing antibiotics doctors are enabling bacteria to develop immunity to these potentially life-saving drugs. There is now no doubt that many of our most useful drugs have been devalued by overuse and are no longer effective.

If your doctor prescribes an antibiotic for you don't be afraid to ask him whether you really need it. He may simply be prescribing the antibiotic because he thinks you will be disappointed if you don't get one.

The overprescribing of antibiotics is not a new phenomenon.

Over a quarter of a century ago, in my first book, *The Medicine Men*, I pointed out that one huge survey had shown that only one third of the patients given antibiotics had infections at all. Other surveys, I explained, had shown that even when patients do have an infection the antibiotic prescribed is usually the wrong one.

Nothing has improved since then. Today's doctors are just as criminally inept as their predecessors were. And members of the medical profession still treat me like a pariah for daring to expose these professional shortcomings.

But it is now clear that the warning about antibiotics which I gave two decades ago was absolutely accurate. The careless, inaccurate and inappropriate prescribing of antibiotics by thousands of ignorant and careless doctors is one of the main reasons why a growing number of bugs are resistant to antibiotic therapy. Many once powerful drugs no longer work because doctors have handed them out like sweeties and bugs have been given the chance to grow stronger and resistant to treatment. An ever increasing number of patients are dying because antibiotics no longer work as well as they used to work.

During the last thirty years I have made scores of predictions about health matters. Most of those predictions were laughed at by the medical establishment when I first made them. Nearly all of them have already come true.

In the first edition of this book (published in 1996) I predicted that infectious diseases would soon become one of the most feared and important causes of death – just as they were before the development of antibiotics. 'This tragic state of affairs will,' I wrote, 'be the fault of those doctors who have overprescribed these drugs.'

Sadly, that prediction has now come true too.

# 7 How Safe Are Repeat Prescriptions?

A growing number of prescriptions (now said to be about half of all those written) are provided without there being any meeting between the doctor and the patient. The patient writes or telephones for a new supply of a specific drug and then, a day or so later, either collects or receives through the post the appropriate prescription.

This system of providing prescriptions 'on request' was originally designed to help patients suffering from chronic disorders such as diabetes, high blood pressure or epilepsy. Patients suffering from disorders which tend to vary very little over the months do not need daily, weekly or even monthly medical examinations but they may need regular supplies of drugs. For them to have to visit a doctor simply to obtain a prescription is clearly a waste of everyone's time. Doctors do not usually prescribe quantities of drugs likely to last more than four to six weeks since some drugs deteriorate if kept too long and most practitioners feel that it is unwise to allow any patient to keep excessively large quantities of drugs at home.

Unfortunately, repeat prescribing is not always restricted to patients with long-term problems requiring continuous medication. Patients who really should see a doctor (rather than simply continue taking tablets) sometimes ask for repeat prescriptions and, to the shame of the medical profession, not infrequently obtain them.

Many patients have become psychologically dependent upon sleeping tablets and tranquillisers because of the ease with which they have been able to obtain repeat prescriptions.

Arrangements for obtaining repeat prescriptions vary a good deal from one doctor's practice to another's. In some practices patients entitled to receive prescriptions are issued with cards on which the drugs which they are allowed to receive without any consultation are listed. There may be a limit on the number of prescriptions which the patient may obtain without being reviewed. In other practices the cards detailing drugs which can be provided on repeat prescriptions are kept with the patient's notes so that the receptionists, who usually write out repeat prescriptions, can check on drugs, and dosages, and make a note of the number of prescriptions used.

Theoretically, doctors signing prescriptions should check all the details, including specific points such as the dosages and quantities of drugs to be supplied, and general points such as the suitability of continuing with the treatment. In practice many prescriptions supplied in this way are signed with few or no checks being made. I have, in the past, obtained evidence that some doctors sign piles of virgin prescription forms and leave their receptionists to fill in the blanks. I have little doubt that this practice continues.

I suggest that patients receiving drugs on repeat prescriptions should always check that the tablets they receive match the tablets previously prescribed, and that any instructions on the bottle label match previous instructions. If there is any confusion or uncertainty then a telephone call should be made to the surgery.

As a general rule, I suggest that only patients who have established and long-term clinical problems should obtain drugs on repeat prescriptions and they should visit the surgery at least once every six months to check that the medication does not need changing. Patients with short-term or acute conditions who need medication should always speak to a doctor.

Repeat prescriptions can be a convenience. But they can lead to drug misuse and eventual abuse – and to addiction and dependence.

# 8 Questions To Ask Before Taking A Prescribed Drug

You will improve your chances of benefiting from a drug – and also minimise the risk of problems – if you know what to expect. You have a right to know what you are taking – and why. Don't be shy. Here are some questions you should ask your doctor:

1. What is this medicine for?
2. How long should I take it? Should I take it until the bottle is empty or until my symptoms have gone?
3. What should I do if I miss a dose?
4. What side effects should I particularly watch out for? Will the medicine make me drowsy?
5. Am I likely to need to take more when these have gone? Should I arrange another consultation?
6. Are there any foods I should avoid? Should I avoid alcohol?
7. How long will the medicine take to work – and how will I know that it is working?

## 9 Don't Let Your Doctor Label You

If, a few years ago, you went to see your doctor complaining that you felt miserable and down in the dumps he would have probably prescribed a harmless tonic, chatted to you for twenty minutes and told you to try and get out and enjoy yourself a bit more.

Today, if you go to see your doctor and complain that you feel under the weather he will probably diagnose you as depressed. There is an excellent chance that he will then start you on one of the many new powerful chemicals now available.

Until the mid 1990s depression was a fairly uncommon disease.

The value of world wide sales of antidepressants rarely rose above $2,500,000,000 a year. (To the world's drug companies that's small change – hardly worth bothering to take to the bank).

But today depression is one of the fastest growing diseases in the world. Millions of people now suffer from it. Astonishingly, 29 per cent of American citizens are now 'officially' mentally ill – many of them suffering from depression. And the boom in the diagnosis of depression has coincided with the development of special, new, expensive, chemical antidepressants.

My fear is that the diagnosis of 'depression' is now often being made when patients are simply rather miserable or unhappy or generally fed up with their lives.

You will not be surprised to hear that although I (well known to be suspicious and rather cynical of the motives of the pharmaceutical industry) worry that some of these new antidepressant drugs may, in due course, prove to produce dangerous or nasty side effects, the majority of doctors are happily prescribing them by the bucket load.

My big fear is that the drugs which are now being prescribed with the enthusiasm which was shown for the benzodiazepine tranquillisers in the 1970s (and, by many doctors, for patients with very similar symptoms) may turn out to produce massive problems of their own.

It may well be true that a relatively small number of depressed patients can be helped by taking drugs.

I have no doubt that people with real depression, who suffer such symptoms as constant crying, an inability to sleep, a total feeling of worthlessness, a loss of appetite, suicidal tendencies or other serious symptoms of depression, need sophisticated, professional help.

But I believe that the amount of good that is being done by these powerful drugs could be far outweighed by the possible harm.

I have absolutely no doubt that there is more sadness, despair, and unhappiness in our society than there has ever been in any previous society but I strongly suspect that many of the patients diagnosed as suffering from 'depression' may well be 'sad' (and suffering from the disorder which I call 'The Twenty-First Century Blues') rather than clinically 'depressed', and may need help of a different kind.

I believe that instead of automatically dosing all their unhappy patients with powerful and potentially hazardous chemicals, and attempting to tackle a vague and ill-defined disease, doctors should be encouraging more of the sad, the despairing and the unhappy to try to tackle the specific causes of their unhappiness themselves. It can be done.

\* \* \*

Depression is not the only disease which is said to be commoner today than it used to be.

Asthma is another disorder which is often said to affect more people now than in the past.

And arthritis is a third disease which is alleged to be getting commoner.

In my view the problem is not that these (and many other) diseases are just becoming commoner, but that doctors are diagnosing them more often.

There is a huge difference.

Take a mild wheeze into a doctor's surgery these days and the chances are that the doctor will tell you that you've got asthma and that you must use an inhaler for the rest of your life.

Complain of an aching joint and you'll be labelled 'arthritic' – and given pills to take.

As a result of this wild, overprescribing policy countless thousands of people who regard themselves as asthmatics, or arthritics are nothing of the sort. They have, in truth, merely exhibited minor, temporary symptoms which do not need long-term treatment.

The driving force behind this vast overprescribing is, in my opinion, the ubiquitous drugs industry.

\* \* \*

The drug companies want doctors to prescribe more medicines (for the simple reason that prescribing more pills pushes up profits even higher) and it is, I believe, their subtle, ever present, overall, global influence which results in doctors deciding that every wheeze must be treated as asthma, that every ache must be diagnosed and treated as 'arthritis' and that every mild bout of unhappiness must be treated as depression.

Diseases such as asthma, arthritis and depression are perfect for making big profits because patients labelled as suffering from these conditions are often advised to take pills for years or even decades.

It is by no means unusual for patients to be told that they need drug therapy for life.

With pills often costing a small fortune the profits on each new patient can be colossal.

This bizarre, ruthless but profitable philosophy works because doctors are usually far too ready to listen to the drug company salesmen. These days most doctors are actually taught about new drugs not by independent experts but by paid salesmen!

My advice is simple: if your doctor tells you that you are suffering from a long-term disorder for which you need to take long-term drug therapy – you should ask for a second opinion.

Never forget that four out of ten patients who take pills suffer side effects. If you are taking pills because you genuinely need them then the risks may be acceptable. But if you are taking pills unnecessarily then the risks are unnecessary too.

## 10 How To Survive In Hospital

Going into hospital is a frightening and worrying experience. The very smell and sound of a hospital is enough to make most people's hearts beat faster.

When we go into hospital we are inevitably nervous about what is going to happen and anxious about the outcome. But on top of those natural fears we worry in case we do something silly or offend someone.

To the outsider hospitals seem full of important looking people in uniforms – all rushing round and all knowing exactly what they are doing.

1. Before you go into hospital try and find out as much as you can about the **rules and regulations** for patients and visitors. Good hospitals produce small booklets for new patients. Get one if you can. If the hospital you're going to doesn't produce a booklet or leaflet of its own then find out as much as you can over the telephone. You need to know when visiting times are; whether there are any special rules about children visiting; what buses stop near to the hospital and what car parking facilities there are for visiting.

2. So that you'll know what to expect find out **what sort of ward** you'll be going into. Open plan wards may seem a little daunting but don't be put off. The evidence shows that nurses can keep a closer eye on patients in large wards than they can when patients are cooped up in private rooms. If your condition is likely to require very special care then you may be put into an Intensive Care Unit or Coronary Care Unit. Children under 12 are usually put onto special children's wards. But older children often go onto adult wards – where they're usually much happier and invariably spoilt rotten by the nurses.

3. Carefully plan **what to take with you**. Here is my basic checklist:

♦ Any pills or medication that you normally take (that includes medicines that you have been prescribed by your doctor, bought yourself or been give by an alternative medicine practitioner).

♦ Any letter of introduction written by your own doctor.

♦ Night clothes, dressing gown and slippers.

♦ Toilet bag with usual contents for an overnight stay.

♦ Small box or pack of paper tissues.

♦ Notepaper, pen and stamps. Coins for the telephone.

♦ Small, silent bedside clock.

♦ Enough money to buy a daily paper.

♦ A couple of books or magazines for light reading.

♦ Make-up bag (for women).

Don't take outdoor clothes or expensive jewellery (including watches) with you.

4. When you go into hospital do remember that however important all the people working there may seem to be **none of them is as important as you are**. They are all employed to look after you.

If you are worried about something, or there is something you don't understand then ask. The best person to ask for advice will probably be the most junior doctor. He or she will have all the information you need and will be on the ward many times during the day. And do remember that although you are in hospital you can still consult your family doctor if you want to. If you are unhappy about a planned operation or treatment programme and you want independent advice from someone you trust then telephone your family doctor and ask for his or her help. He or she can visit you in hospital, talk to your doctors and read your notes.

## 11 Watch Out For Side Effects

Whenever your doctor gives you a drug to take it is vitally important that you watch out for side effects. Four out of ten people who are given drugs by their doctors will suffer uncomfortable, hazardous or even lethal side effects.

Drugs which are highly promoted when they are launched but which are eventually shown to be totally useless often cause illnesses far worse than the complaint for which they were prescribed. Far more people are killed by prescription drugs than are killed by illegal drugs such as heroin and cocaine.

The incidence of side effects is now so widespread that it is generally accepted by most doctors that if a patient who is receiving treatment for one condition develops a new symptom then the chances are that the new symptom will have been caused by the treatment for the original problem. And as I have pointed out on many occasions no less than one in six hospital patients are there because they have been made ill by their doctor.

Perhaps the most convincing evidence of the failure of our current drug testing systems to protect patients lies in the number of drugs which have had to be withdrawn after they have been passed as 'safe' by the authorities. I know of over 80 drugs which have had to be withdrawn or restricted because they were considered to be too dangerous for widespread use. Some of these drugs were withdrawn after months. Others were taken off the market after being sold for years.

Can you imagine the outcry if testing methods were so inadequate that 80 types of motor car or 80 varieties of food had to be withdrawn because they were found to be unsafe?

Doctors, the drug industry and the government all claim that nothing can be done to avoid this drug scandal. I don't believe this is true. If governments really wanted to protect patients there are many things they could do.

Since the end of the 1970s I have argued that we need an international, computerised drug monitoring service – designed to make sure that doctors in one part of the world know when doctors in other countries have spotted problems. Astonishingly, no such system exists.

You might imagine that when a drug is withdrawn in one country other countries will take similar action. But you would be wrong. One drug that was officially withdrawn in the USA and France was not officially withdrawn in the UK until five years later.

I believe that one of the main reasons for the international epidemic of drug-induced illness is the greed of the big international drug companies. They make a fortune out of making and selling drugs and their ruthlessness and levels of profit make the arms industry look like a church charity.

Governments could dramatically reduce the incidence of lethal, dangerous and uncomfortable side effects by insisting that drugs be extensively tested before being prescribed for millions of people around the world. At the moment drugs can be launched onto the mass market after relatively few tests have been done. The authorities admit that they don't know what side effects will be produced until a drug has been on the market for a while.

And patients would be far, far safer if drug companies were stopped from testing drugs on animals. Pharmaceutical companies love to test drugs on animals because they can't lose. If the animal tests show that the drug doesn't produce side effects in animals the company will proclaim the drug 'safe' and put it on the market. But if the animal tests show that the drug causes side effects the company will dismiss the results as irrelevant – and put the drug on the market anyway – because animals are different to people.

If you have ever suffered unpleasant side effects the chances are high that the drug you were given was tested on animals. The evidence available now shows that animal experiments are so misleading and inaccurate that they result in many human deaths. Here are three case histories which show that animal experiments kill people:

1. Eight-year-old Samantha loved ballet dancing passionately. She

wanted to be a ballet dancer when she grew up. But she never did grow up. Ten days before her ninth birthday she fell ill. Her ballet class was holding a public performance on the following Saturday and she desperately wanted to be well enough to appear so her mother took her along to see their family doctor. Within 48 hours Samantha was dead: killed not by the illness but by the drug she'd been given. The drug had been tested but most of the early tests had been done on animals. These had not shown the side effect which killed Samantha.

2. Forty-four-year old Robert failed a routine life assurance examination, carried out so that he could take out a new and larger mortgage on a house he and his wife had bought. He felt well but his doctor insisted on treating him. The drug he was given had been extensively tested on animals. Unexpected side effects produced by the drug resulted in his death three weeks later.

3. Bill was in pain. Doctors recommended surgery. The surgeon he saw wanted to try out a new technique that had been tested on animals. Bill died three days after the operation. He developed problems and complications which had not occurred when the operation had been performed on animals.

All these human tragedies occurred as a direct result of animal experiments. In all these case histories the identifying facts have been changed to protect the privacy of the families concerned. It isn't only animals who suffer from 'animal testing'. People suffer too. No animal experiment has ever saved a human life, but animal experiments have resulted in many deaths.

My books *Why Animal Experiments Must Stop* and *Betrayal of Trust* contain more information about the use of animals in experiments and are available free on my website www.vernoncoleman.com.

\* \* \*

Despite the fact that one must hold the pharmaceutical industry directly responsible for most of the side effects (and deaths) caused by drugs there is no doubt that the number of problems could be reduced if patients were more aware of how best to protect themselves from side effects.

It is a sad but true fact that of all the drugs prescribed only a relatively small number are taken in the way that the prescriber originally intended them to be taken. Drugs are taken at the wrong time, they are taken too frequently and they are sometimes never taken out of the bottle at all.

It is important to remember that modern prescribed drugs are not only potentially effective but also powerful and potentially dangerous.

There are several questions which should be answered before a patient starts taking a drug – for example, how long the drug should be taken for, whether it should be taken before, during or after meals and whether it can cause drowsiness. Usually the answers to these questions will appear on the label of the bottle containing the drugs. If the answers do not appear there then the fault may lie with the doctor who wrote the prescription or the pharmacist who dispensed it.

Here are some things to watch out for:

1.  Some drugs can be stopped when symptoms cease. Others need to be taken as a complete course. A small number of drugs need to be taken continuously and a second prescription will have to be obtained before the first supply has run out. The patient who knows what his drug is for, why he is taking it and what the effect should be, will be more likely to know when a drug is to be stopped.

2.  If a drug has to be taken once a day, it is usually important that it is taken at the same time each day. If a drug has to be taken twice a day it should be taken at intervals of 12 hours. A drug that needs to be taken three times a day should be taken at eight-hourly intervals and a drug that needs taking four times a day should be taken at six-hourly intervals. The day should be divided into suitable segments.

3.  Some drugs which may cause stomach problems are safer when taken with meals. Other drugs may not be absorbed properly if taken with food.

4.  A number of patients (particularly the elderly) are expected to remember to take dozens of pills a day. When a day's medication includes tablets to be taken twice daily, three times daily, mornings only and every four hours, mistakes are inevitable. If a patient needs to take a number of drugs a day mistakes can be minimised by preparing a daily chart on which the names and times of different drugs are marked. Such a chart will reduce the risk of a patient taking one dose twice or struggling to remember whether

a particular pill has been taken yet. To avoid the risk of overdosage, sleeping tablets should not be kept by the bedside. It is too easy for a half-asleep patient to mistakenly take extra tablets. In the case of a suspected overdose medical attention must be sought.

\* \* \*

Here is a list of some possible, common side effects:

1. Drowsiness is a common problem with all drugs which have an effect on the central nervous system – these include sedatives, tranquillisers, sleeping pills, most drugs used in the treatment of anxiety and depression and drugs used in the treatment of epilepsy. Drowsiness is also common with antihistamines (these are commonly used for allergies and so patients suffering from hayfever, for example, should be aware that their medication may make them feel sleepy).

2. Nausea and vomiting may be caused by many different drugs including pain relievers, drugs used to treat infections, hormones and drugs prescribed for heart conditions.

3. Dizziness is commonly caused by aspirin but drugs used to treat high blood pressure, nerve disorders such as anxiety and depression and infections can also cause this side effect.

4. Drugs such as penicillin which are used to treat infections often cause diarrhoea – as do some drugs prescribed for intestinal disorders such as indigestion, gastritis and constipation.

5. Headache is a symptom that is associated with an enormous range of drugs.

6. Drugs used in the treatment of high blood pressure and in the treatment of nerve problems seem particularly likely to produce a dry mouth.

7. Pain relievers, drugs used to treat infections and steroid drugs are the prescription products which seem most likely to cause indigestion or wind.

8. Skin rashes are extremely common among patients taking drugs. Drugs used to treat infections – such as penicillin and sulphonamide – are commonly associated with this problem. A skin rash may suggest an allergy to a drug.

9. Itching associated with a skin rash means that an allergy reaction is almost certain.

10. Constipation is a common side effect with pain relievers, antacids, cough medicines and (naturally enough) drugs used in the treatment of diarrhoea.

11. Other side effects which are commonly noticed by patients taking prescription drugs include: confusion, hallucinations, tremors, fainting, wheezing, palpitations, blurred vision, depression, sweating, ringing in the ears and sexual problems such as frigidity and impotence.

\* \* \*

Here are some tips to help you minimise your risk of developing a side effect if you have to take a prescription drug.

1. Always follow any specific instructions that you have been given by your doctor. Read the label on your bottle of pills and take notice of what it says.

2. When you're not using them drugs should be stored in a locked cupboard out of reach of children, in a room where the temperature will be fairly stable. The bathroom is probably the worst room in the house for storing medicines. Your bedroom – which probably has a more stable temperature – is much better.

3. Never take drugs which were prescribed for someone else. Return all unused supplies of drugs to your pharmacist.

4. It is wise to assume that all prescribed drugs can cause drowsiness. You shouldn't drive or operate machinery after taking a drug until you are sure that you are safe.

5. Drugs do not mix well with alcohol. If you want to drink while taking drugs ask your doctor whether or not it will be safe.

6. Do not take non-prescribed medicines while taking prescribed drugs unless your doctor has told you that you can.

7. Do not stop taking drugs suddenly if you have been advised to take a full course. Ring your doctor for advice if you need to stop for any reason. Some drugs have to be stopped gradually rather than abruptly.

8. Be on the look out for side effects and remember that if you seem

to develop new symptoms while taking a prescription drug then the chances are high that the new symptoms were caused by the treatment you are taking for your original symptoms.

9. Report any side effects to your doctor – and ask him if he's going to report the side effects to the authorities. The vast majority of doctors never bother to report side effects – with the result that potentially hazardous drugs remain on the market for far longer than they should.

10. If you need to see a doctor while taking a drug make sure he knows what you are taking – particularly if he intends to prescribe new treatment for you. Many drugs do not mix well together and may, indeed, react together in a dangerous way.

11. Do not assume that a doctor you have seen in the past will remember what he prescribed for you on a previous occasion.

12. Learn the names and purposes of the drugs you take. If you are not sure when to take the drugs that you have been given ask your doctor or the pharmacist. If you think you will forget the instructions you are given ask for them to be written down. The name of the drug should always appear on the container.

13. Do not remove drugs from their proper containers except when you need them or if you are transferring them to a device intended to improve compliance.

14. Try to see the same doctor as often as possible. If several doctors are prescribing for you there may be an increased risk of an interaction between drugs which do not mix well.

15. Use drugs with care and caution, but do use them when they are required. Doctors sometimes divide patients into two main groups: those who are willing to take drugs for any little symptom and who feel deprived if not offered a pharmacological solution to every ailment, and those who are unwilling to take drugs under any circumstances. Try not to fall into either of these extreme groups.

# 12 Should You Get A Second Opinion?

Many patients automatically trust their doctor – assuming that he or she must always be right. But that can be a deadly mistake.

It has always been diagnostic skills which have differentiated between the good doctor and the bad doctor. Treating sick people is easy. If you are a doctor and you know what is wrong with your patient you can look up the correct treatment in two minutes. Sadly, however, many doctors seem to have lost their abilities to diagnose accurately.

1. When researchers examined the medical records of 100 dead patients who had been shown by post mortem to have had heart attacks they found that only 53 per cent of the heart attacks had been diagnosed. What makes this even more alarming is the fact that half the patients had been looked after by experts in heart disease.

2. A study of 32 hospitals which compared the diagnoses doctors had made when treating 1,800 patients, with the diagnoses made after the patients had died (and could be examined more thoroughly), showed that doctors had an error rate of nearly 20 per cent.

3. A study of 131 randomly selected psychiatric patients showed that approximately three quarters (75 per cent) of the patients may have been wrongly diagnosed.

4. In many cases patients are diagnosed as having – and are then treated for – serious psychiatric problems when their symptoms are caused by drugs they have been given for physical problems. Whole wards full of patients have been diagnosed, treated and classified as schizophrenic when in fact they were suffering from

side effects produced by the drugs they had been given by prescription-happy doctors.

5.  When 80 doctors were asked to examine silicone models of female breasts they could only find half the hidden lumps. A 50 per cent failure rate even though the doctors knew that they were being tested and observed.

6.  Another study showed that doctors had missed diagnoses in dying patients up to a quarter of the time. Experts concluded that one in ten patients who had died would have lived if the correct diagnosis had been made.

7.  Another study revealed that in two thirds of patients who had died, important, previously undiagnosed conditions were discovered in the post mortem room.

8.  A report published after pathologists had performed 400 post mortem examinations showed that in more than half the cases the wrong diagnosis had been made. The authors of this report said that potentially treatable disease was missed in 13 per cent of patients; that 65 out of 134 cases of pneumonia had gone undetected and that out of 51 patients who had suffered heart attacks doctors had failed to diagnose the problem in 18 cases.

All this is terrifying. For if the doctor doesn't make the right diagnosis then it doesn't matter how many wonderful drugs he has at his disposal.

There are many reasons why today's doctors are so bad at making the correct diagnosis.

Education is often lamentable – with lecturers too often teaching medical students about organs and tissues rather than living patients, and then examining them on their ability to remember huge lists of details about bones, blood vessels and pathology details without ever testing them on their ability to use the information they have acquired.

And studies have shown that doctors are at their worst when dealing with patients with whom they feel uncomfortable. Narrow training means that doctors feel uncomfortable with a wide range of people. They often have difficulty relating to, talking to or acquiring information from people of 'different' races, sexes or social backgrounds.

An even bigger problem is the fact that modern doctors rely far too much on technology – and far too little on building up any diagnostic skills of their own.

Old-fashioned doctors used to rely on what their patients told them and on what their own eyes, ears, noses and fingertips told them. Most important of all, perhaps, was the sixth sense that doctors used to acquire through years of clinical experience.

Modern doctors rely too much upon equipment which is often faulty, frequently badly calibrated and more often than not downright misleading.

For example, nearly every published study on the subject puts the error rate for doctors reading X-rays at between 20 per cent and 40 per cent. Radiologists working at a big hospital disagreed on the interpretation of chest radiographs as much as 56 per cent of the time. And there were potentially significant errors in 41 per cent of their reports. Even when X-rays are read for a second time only about a third of the initial errors are spotted.

So, the lesson here is a very simple one: do not automatically assume that your doctor's diagnosis must be right. If you are at all unhappy about the diagnosis – and feel that your doctor could be wrong – insist on a second opinion.

## 13 Is Your Doctor Really Qualified?

In America a hoax psychiatrist persuaded 10 married women to have sex with total strangers. He telephoned the women at random and claimed to be a psychiatrist secretly treating their husbands for sexual problems. He told them that they should leave the house and come back with the first man they could find and await further instructions. In a second call he told the women – and the strangers they'd brought home – to have sex. He claimed it would help cure the husband's problem. Ten per cent of the women who'd been telephoned followed the hoaxer's instructions.

In Italy a hospital found that one of its top brain surgeons wasn't even qualified as a doctor. In England a meat salesman performed 14 operations in just 24 days while a biology teacher posed as a gynaecologist for six months before getting caught.

Fake doctors are commoner than you might imagine. In recent years I have reported many extraordinary (but true) stories of unqualified doctors convincing both patients and medical colleagues about their authenticity.

So if you have any doubts at all about whether or not your doctor is properly qualified go to your local library and check him out.

# 14 DON'T LET YOUR DOCTOR CONDEMN YOU TO DEATH

It is customary in developed, sophisticated countries to regard voodoo as primitive and mildly amusing. We feel comfortably able to scoff at the idea of anyone dying because a man in a grass skirt, with paint on his face and chicken feathers on his head, tells him that he is going to die. We feel secure in the knowledge that such threats would never work on us.

And yet, in our own way, we are just as vulnerable as any primitive native who succumbs to the power and influence of a malevolent witch doctor.

The difference is merely that instead of listening to, and believing, curses pronounced by men wearing grass skirts and chicken feathers we listen, believe and respond to the allegedly scientifically based prognoses announced by men wearing white coats.

If a doctor in a white coat tells a man that he is going to die, that man will probably die.

I know a man who was told, several years ago, that he was dying of cancer. He lost weight, became unable to move and started to die.

And then, as he lay in bed quietly and obediently waiting to die, his wife took a telephone call from the hospital. There had, said a voice, been a mistake. Her husband did not have cancer at all. He had a treatable infection. There had been a mix up in the laboratory.

When told this good news the man made a miraculous recovery. He stopped dying because he no longer expected to die.

The evidence confirms that things like this happen regularly. Patients listen to doctors – and take notice of what they are told. And so the doctors' predictions come true – whether or not they are accurate.

Whether the information comes from a man dressed in feathers with a string of beads around his neck, or from a man in a white coat with a stethoscope around his neck, it is faith that does the damage.

If the individual on the receiving end of the spell or bad news believes what he is told, his imagination will do the rest. Patients – however intelligent or sophisticated they consider themselves – can sink into a steady decline through their own attitude, without input from anyone else. They can convince themselves that they are going to die. And then they will turn their heads to the wall and prepare themselves for death.

All this is frightening and disturbing.

But there is another way of looking at the power of the imagination.

For just as patients have died because they have believed that they are dying, so patients have survived and bloomed because they have refused to accept the bad news that they have been given.

Just as fear and anxiety can kill, so hope and determination can delay death.

By harnessing their inner strength, and the power of their imaginations, individuals who have been told that they are soon to die have succeeded in cheating death.

We all have powers of which too few of us are aware. We should use them.

(I have explored the powers of the mind at greater length – and with many practical examples – in my book *Mindpower*).

## 15   WHY MENTAL HEALTH CARE ISN'T ALWAYS WORTH HAVING

Most people think that mental illness is something that happens to other people; something that touches other people's families. It isn't.

The number of people suffering from mental illness is rising continuously and rapidly. Nearly one in three American citizens have been diagnosed as suffering from mental illness. In most countries between 10 per cent and 15 per cent of the entire population suffer, at some stage in their lives, from mental illness severe enough to warrant their admission to a mental hospital.

Think of eight or nine people you know: the chances are that one person in any group of eight or nine will either have already spent time in a mental hospital or will, in the future, need to spend time in a mental hospital.

All that is frightening enough.

But what really frightens me is the fact that today the treatment of patients with psychiatric problems is at best ineffective and at worst barbaric. Twenty first century psychiatry is more of a black art than a science and I believe the majority of mentally ill patients would be better off if all the psychiatrists were banished to Siberia.

We think of psychiatry as a scientific discipline but I think it is based more on rumour, suspicion and gossip than on science. Here are some facts that you should know about the way mental illness is treated today.

### 1. Brain Surgery

Surgeons have operated on the brains of thousands of mental patients in the last 40 or so years. They have made cuts in the brain and chopped bits out of the brain. But I have never been able to find any real evidence to show that brain surgery does any good for mental illness. One experienced psychiatrist, who now regrets having referred patients for psychosurgery, has compared it to 'pulling the wires out of a TV set in an attempt to get a better picture'. In the 1960s many doctors recommended psychosurgery enthusiastically. By 1974 the World Health Organisation was getting very critical about brain surgery for mental illness. WHO experts decided that: 'the procedures in contemporary psychosurgery are based on inadequate or limited research and they entail many hazards. Psychosurgery has unpredictable effects...'.

You might have thought that would have been that. Not a bit of it. There are still doctors around who believe that mentally ill patients can be helped by having knives stuck into their brains.

### 2. Psychotherapy
You don't have to be a doctor to be a psychotherapist. Anyone can describe himself or herself as a psychotherapist. My cat Alice was one of the most highly qualified psychotherapists in the world.

What do psychotherapists do? Good question. Basically, they listen to (and occasionally talk to) their patients.

Do they do any good? I don't think so.

I suspect that a chat to a hairdresser or to a barman will do a patient as much good as a chat to a psychotherapist and that patients who are treated with psychotherapy are slightly more likely to become mentally ill, become alcoholics or commit a major crime than are patients who get no psychotherapy.

In my view, lots of psychotherapists are nutters. Many charge ridiculously high fees. Few do any good. Some should be locked up.

### 3. Electroconvulsive Therapy (ECT)
When we look back a couple of hundred years we tend to be rather critical about the way that the mentally ill were treated in those long off dim and distant days. At the Bethlem Royal Hospital in London in 1770 you could have paid a penny to watch the depressed and the manic being bled, beaten, soaked in cold water and blasted with electricity.

Terrible.

We don't do that.

Do we?

Well, we may no longer deliberately beat or bleed the mentally ill (not officially at least) but we do still blast them with electricity. Electroconvulsive therapy is still used by a large number of psychiatrists as a 'treatment' for mentally ill patients.

Doctors have been using electricity as a therapy for centuries. In ancient Rome, Scriborus Largus, tried to cure the emperor's headache with an electric eel. But it was in 1938 that the use of electricity for the 'treatment' of mental illness was 'rediscovered'. Two Italians, called Cerletti and Bini, decided to try pumping fairly large amounts of electricity into the human brain to treat schizophrenia. They developed Electroconvulsive Therapy (ECT) because they believed that epilepsy and schizophrenia could not exist together. (ECT is, of course, a sort of artificially induced epileptic attack.)

In a standard ECT session electrodes are attached to one or both sides of the patient's head and something like 80 to 100 volts are applied to the head for up to a second at a time. That amount of electricity provides a big enough current to light up a 100 watt light bulb. Not surprisingly, perhaps, in a human being it causes a brain seizure which can be traced on an electroencephalogram.

While being given the treatment patients are usually anaesthetised and given a muscle relaxant. Without the muscle relaxant contractions can be so severe that bones can be fractured or teeth chipped. An electrocardiogram is sometimes used to monitor the beating of the heart and some doctors give oxygen to reduce the risk of brain damage. (From all this you may begin to get the idea that ECT isn't exactly a risk free procedure.)

After the electric shock has been given, patients slowly regain consciousness but usually remain groggy and confused for a while. Sometimes patients complain that their ability to remember events from the past has disappeared. Author Ernest Hemingway was convinced that ECT erased his personal experiences and ruined his career as a writer.

For thirty years or so after Cerletti and Bini introduced ECT psychiatrists all around the world continued to use the 'therapy', apparently without worrying too much about such minor inconveniences as the lack of evidence to show that it worked.

Psychiatry is very much a black art and ECT is almost certainly the blackest of the black art therapies.

By the 1960s there was growing disquiet about this type of treatment. Despite a lack of convincing evidence showing that pumping electricity into the brain did any good, a number of experts had decided that it could do harm. Many patients told how they had been held down or tied down and given huge doses of electricity which had sent them into violent convulsions. It all sounded terribly barbaric – more like something from a mediaeval torture chamber than a twentieth century hospital.

Then, in 1975 the film *One Flew Over The Cuckoo's Nest* was released. In the book, based on Ken Kesey's book, actor Jack Nicholson was seen receiving electric shock treatment. This reinforced the idea that electric shock therapy was cruel, barbaric and outdated. The amount of public pressure on doctors to stop giving electric shocks to psychiatric patients increased for a while.

But then psychiatrists started to argue that they had nothing else to offer in the place of ECT. And the popularity of the technique began to rise once more.

However, there was still confusion and controversy about just how ECT should be applied and which patients it might help. Numerous experiments had been done – including some at Buchenwald during the Second World War – but there was still no agreement on how to get the best out of the alleged treatment.

The controversy and confusion was, I feel, summarised well in a paper entitled 'Indications for Electric-Convulsive Therapy and Its Use by Senior Psychiatrists' that was written by two psychiatrists and published in the *British Medical Journal* back in the late 1970s.

The authors sent a questionnaire to a number of senior psychiatrists and, as a result, showed that there was a considerable difference of opinion among psychiatrists about how best the treatment could be used.

First, there were great differences in the frequency with which psychiatrists used ECT. Some referred ten to twenty patients a month for ECT. One said he never used it.

Second, the survey also showed that there were significant differences between the reasons given for using ECT. Some psychiatrists said they thought it was useful in the treatment of depression. Some said they used it for schizophrenia. Some said they found it useful for mania.

Third, the researchers found that more than a third of the consultants believed that temporary memory loss was invariably associated with clinically effective ECT. Despite this – and other risks associated with the treatment – less than 20 per cent of the consultants personally administered ECT. Most preferred to leave this unpleasant work to junior members of their staffs.

But the most startling conclusion was that psychiatrists still did not agree about how to apply ECT. Some consultants said that they preferred to give four treatments. Others preferred a series of twelve treatments. Some of the consultants placed the electrodes on one side of the head. Other consultants placed the electrodes on both sides of the head. I would not be surprised to read that some had their patients sit in a bath of cold custard.

It seemed to me, when I first read it, that this startling survey strongly suggested that psychiatrists applying ECT didn't have the faintest idea what they are doing.

The disquiet produced by this study led to a major report on ECT published by the UK's Royal College of Psychiatrists (RCP) in 1981. This report was based on 2,755 questionnaires completed by doctors using ECT. The RCP report pointed out that of the 100 clinics where the researchers watched ECT being given not one satisfied the standards that the RCP had outlined. The RCP report also claimed that obsolete machinery was being used.

As a result the UK Secretary of State for Social Services set up a working group which concluded that although over 20,000 ECT treatments were being given every year in the UK there was 'no agreed theoretical basis for the use of particular wave forms, frequencies, energy, rate of delivery of energy, etc.' and so there were 'no minimal performance requirements for the effective and safe use of ECT equipment to guide ECT equipment manufacturers'. In other words, it seemed that after well over four decades of use, doctors did not know how ECT worked, they did not know which patients it should be given to, they did not know how it should be applied and they did not know how best to make the equipment to give the electric shocks. Hardly a rousing vote of confidence for ECT or psychiatry.

Again, this study showed that psychiatrists couldn't agree about which patients should be treated with ECT. Some psychiatrists who used ECT claimed that it was most useful in the treatment of severe depression. Some said it was appropriate for schizophrenia. Some said it wasn't. Some were probably in two minds about it.

The survey done by the Royal College of Psychiatrists showed that very few doctors seemed to know where the electrodes should be applied and in three quarters of the clinics visited by the doctors organising the survey for the RCP the settings on the machines used to give ECT were never altered, even though ECT machines were made so that the strength and pulse of the current given could be varied according to the illness and particular needs of each individual patient. (The snag, of course, was that although these things could be altered no one seemed to know *how* they should be altered.)

Some machines available had no automatic timer so that the control of the dose of electricity given depended entirely on the operator. (Despite the fact that too much ECT is known to lead to prolonged memory impairment). It was even found that only about half the ECT equipment in regular use received any regular maintenance. Why bother to maintain a machine when you don't even know what the damned thing is supposed to do?

I have been vehemently critical of ECT for decades. It has always seemed to me to be a primitive, barbaric and crude form of 'therapy'. As a medical student I once had to watch it being administered. I remember feeling deeply ashamed of the profession I was preparing to enter.

In 1988, in my book *The Health Scandal* I wrote that: 'Every year tens of thousands of patients receive a form of treatment that still hasn't been properly tested. No one has any idea why it should work, or indeed if it works. No one knows the extent of the damage it can do. No one knows when it should be given or when it should be avoided at all costs. No one knows what sort of machinery should be used or what dosage of electricity should be given. No one really knows where the electrodes should be applied.'

Over a quarter of a century ago a wise psychiatrist told me that in his view blasting electricity into the brain (an organ about which we understand little more now than we knew then) was about as rational, as scientific and as logical as blasting 30,000 volts into a malfunctioning TV set.

But, despite all the controversy, thousands of psychiatrists still use ECT to 'treat' their patients. Shocking? Of course it is.

The fact that ECT is still used at all is a disgrace to psychiatry and to the medical profession as a whole. A psychiatrist who attacks his patients with such a bizarre and unscientific form of pseudo-therapy is, in my opinion, not to be trusted.

## 16 | How To Protect Yourself Against Bugs

If you think that bugs are just wishy-washy bugs that cause flu, tummy upsets and other relatively minor inconveniences – think again.

Infectious diseases are now a major threat to your health – and your family's health.

There are several main reasons why infectious diseases are back.

First, international air travel means that killer bugs can be brought from the jungle to the city within hours. There was far less danger when infected individuals travelled on slower, more traditional forms of transport. Patients carrying the disease would have died long before they reached heavily populated cities.

Second, bugs such as viruses are constantly changing – and getting stronger. As scientists produce new vaccines, existing viruses adapt and change. The deadly Ebola virus used to be transmitted through the blood. But changes to the virus in a laboratory means it can now spread through the air – like flu. In 1918-19 a flu bug far less deadly than the Ebola virus killed 25 million people. Genetic engineers experiment with viruses (sometimes for military purposes) and produce new, stronger, more lethal infections.

Third, vivisectors in laboratories around the world are constantly giving existing viruses to animals. They use some of the rarest and most deadly viruses. Some of the research work is done for the military – who want ever more lethal viruses for biological warfare. Problems really start when viruses – or infected animals – escape from laboratories. There are countless billions of viruses in the world – each one a thousandth the size of a bacterium. Every one could be a ticking time bomb.

Fourth, the overprescribing and abuse of antibiotics means that bugs have acquired immunity and have become stronger and more lethal.

Here is what you can do to help protect yourself and your family from killer bugs:

1.  Your body's immune system helps to protect you against infection. If your immune system – your inbuilt defence system – is in tip-top condition then you will be far less vulnerable to these marauding bugs. What you choose to eat can have a big effect on the strength and effectiveness of your immune system. You can strengthen your immune system – and reduce your susceptibility to infections (and cancer) by changing your diet. You must do everything you can to keep your body's immune system in tip-top condition. It is vital to eat regular supplies of foods which contain antioxidants. Recommended foods include: apples, asparagus, baked beans, broccoli, brown rice, Brussels sprouts, cabbage, cauliflower, chick peas, corn, grapefruit, lentils, oats, oranges, peas, pineapples, potatoes, soya beans, spinach, strawberries. I also recommend taking sunflower and pumpkin seeds daily.

2.  Unless your diet naturally contains garlic then I recommend that you take a garlic supplement every day.

3.  If you eat meat it is important that you give it up – particularly if you have an infection which is being treated with antibiotics. The spread of a number of killer infections has been traced to meat shipments. The basic cause is simple: farmers routinely feed antibiotics to their animals to keep them healthy. Animals which are fed with antibiotics inevitably acquire antibiotic resistant organisms. Repeated problems caused by meat infected with antibiotic resistant E. Coli are a direct result of this still unregulated and uncontrolled farming practice. Many of the people who fall ill after eating infected meat have been taking antibiotics – for throat or ear infections for example. The antibiotic prescribed for the throat or ear infection clears the body of many of its natural infections, allowing the antibiotic resistant superbug to take over a virtually competitor free body.

4.  Stress will damage your immune system and impair your body's ability to fight infection. It is, therefore, important that you reduce your exposure to unnecessary stress. Make a list of all the factors which add stress to your life and then avoid those stresses which can be avoided.

5. Try to avoid buildings which have closed circuit air conditioning systems. When air is constantly recirculated your chances of acquiring an infection are dramatically increased. If one person sneezes or coughs then the chances are high that everyone in the building will be exposed to the bug.

6. You should try to keep away from hospitals, doctors' clinics and other places where sick people congregate – and where antibiotic resistant bugs are likely to be much in control. I used to favour open plan wards (as designed by Florence Nightingale) since patients in such wards can be kept constantly under supervision by nurses. The explosion in the incidence of antibiotic resistant bugs means that single rooms are now preferable for any patient requiring hospital treatment.

7. Whenever possible you should avoid methods of public transport which recirculate used air. Modern trains tend to have no opening windows – with the result that if one person sneezes in a carriage the chances are that everyone else will be exposed to (and possibly catch their disease).

8. If you eat eggs do not ever buy (or eat) eggs with cracked shells. It is much easier for an infection to enter an egg with a cracked shell. Eggs laid by genuinely free range chickens are likely to be healthier than eggs laid by hens kept in battery cages.

9. Make sure that your fridge is kept cold enough. The temperature inside your fridge should be below 3 degrees Centigrade.

10. Make sure that you wash your hands thoroughly before preparing food. Staphylococcus, for example, can be transmitted hand to hand. Wash all kitchen dishes and cutlery thoroughly in hot, soapy water.

11. Never refreeze food which has been previously frozen and then thawed. Thawing increases the number of bacteria and refreezing food increases the chances of infection.

12. If you eat meat make sure that it is completely thawed before you start to cook it. If you do not do this then the chances are that the middle of the meat will still be frozen when you start to cook it – and will not be properly cooked when the rest of the meat is ready. Meat which is raw will probably be full of bugs.

13. Keep foods apart from one another in your fridge in order to reduce the risk of cross contamination. Put meat (a high risk source of infection) at the bottom of the fridge and keep it away from other foods.

14. Don't ever buy tins which are rusty, bulging or badly damaged.

15. Always check the sell-by date before buying food. Don't be tempted to buy (or use) food which has passed its sell-by date.

16. If your doctor wants to prescribe an antibiotic ask him if he thinks it is really essential – or if he is just giving you the prescription because he thinks you want an antibiotic. Don't take these drugs unless you really need them.

17. Eat live yoghurt – which contains the 'friendly' lactobacillus acidophilus. (Soya yoghurt also contains it).

18. Don't take drugs (either prescribed or bought over the pharmacy counter) unless you really need them. Always investigate other ways to deal with health problems.

19. Teach children not to cough or sneeze without using a handkerchief.

20. Try not to touch your eyes with your fingers – that's an easy way for bugs to get into your body.

See my book *Superbody* for more advice on this subject.

## 17 | CONQUER HEART DISEASE WITHOUT PILLS OR SURGERY

When I first started writing a syndicated column about medical matters several decades ago I got into a great deal of trouble for daring to suggest that some patients with high blood pressure might be able to reduce their need for pills (maybe entirely) by making some fundamental lifestyle changes.

I recommended losing weight, giving up smoking, avoiding too much stress, learning how to relax, cutting out fatty foods and so on and although I had only been qualified for a year or two this advice seemed to me to be extremely sensible, straightforward and non-controversial. After all, I remember arguing, if stress and fat rich foods can cause high blood pressure then surely a lifestyle which involves learning how to deal with stress and avoiding fatty foods must help reduce high blood pressure.

Today this advice is pretty widely accepted as sound, sensible and effective. Most doctors who have a rudimentary understanding of medicine and whose thinking has not been entirely influenced by the unsubtle promotions of the drugs industry acknowledge that many patients with high blood pressure can avoid drug therapy by following these simple guidelines.

At the time, however, I was regarded as a dangerous heretic. I remember that one eminent doctor, undoubtedly a pillar of the medical establishment, wrote to one of the newspapers which carried my column expressing the view that drug therapy was the only remedy for high blood pressure and that if I had expressed such an opinion in his hospital he would have stopped me practising. Other pillars of the medical establishment sent similarly indignant letters and my column was quickly dropped by several editors who felt that the advice I was offering was too far out of touch with mainstream medicine to be acceptable.

The irony was, I feel now, that safe, sensible, effective advice was being censored because it was simple, because it consisted of too much common sense and not enough high technology and because it did not offer the all powerful pharmaceutical industry any commercial opportunities. (Over the years I have been 'fired' by well over forty local newspapers for having the effrontery to question accepted medical wisdom and antagonise local members of the medical establishment.)

This was, I think, my first experience of being described as 'controversial' for proposing a course of action which seemed to me to be fundamentally sound. The sad bottom line is that I suspect that the lifestyle solution to high blood pressure attracted criticism because it offered no possibility for profit.

A similar situation has developed with regard to the treatment of heart disease.

Most patients and nearly all doctors regard surgery and drug therapy as the only two ways to treat heart problems. Triple and quadruple bypass operations are now almost commonplace – and a major source of revenue for surgeons around the world. There are over 60 different pharmaceutical products available for the treatment of heart problems and many of these are among the world's best selling and most profitable drugs. Doctors who make their living with a scalpel tend to recommend surgery for every heart patient they see whereas doctors who make their living with a pen and a prescription pad are more likely to recommend drug therapy.

To say the least the consequences of all this surgery and this epidemic of prescribing are not always ideal. The unavoidable fact is that giving an anaesthetic, chopping open the chest and physically assaulting the delicate tissues of someone with a dodgy heart is a risky business which results in thousands of deaths every year. As always the irony is that in order to survive hospitalisation and surgery you really need to be in tip-top condition.

Pills aren't necessarily safe either. There are always risks with drugs and powerful drugs which have an effect on the heart can produce damaging, uncomfortable and sometimes lethal side effects. And, of course, it's worth remembering that many heart patients have to undergo surgery *and* take drugs. Indeed, the nearest the medical establishment ever gets to a 'holistic' approach is to offer surgery and pills.

But the good news is that there is evidence now available to show that surgery and drug therapy are not the only ways to tackle heart disease.

It has, of course, been known for some time that it is possible to prevent heart disease by changing your lifestyle. Family history is a major factor in the development of heart trouble and you can't do much about your parents or grandparents. But whether you come from a line of people with healthy hearts or vulnerable, fragile hearts you can dramatically improve your chances of avoiding cardiac trouble by following such simple rules as avoiding fatty foods, taking regular, gentle exercise, learning how to cope with stress and keeping as far away from tobacco as possible.

The recent breakthrough (made largely through the work of an American doctor called Dr Dean Ornish) has been to show that it is actually possible to treat patients with existing heart disease by encouraging them to make significant changes in the way they live. Dr Ornish was the first clinician to provide documented proof that heart disease can be halted or even reversed simply by a change in life-style. After one year the majority (82 per cent) of the patients who made the comprehensive lifestyle changes recommended by Dr Ornish showed some measurable reversal of their coronary artery blockages.

In a regime which is, it seems to me, a perfect example of holistic medicine in practice, Dr Ornish and his colleagues have shown that by persuading patients to follow some simple basic rules – which include taking half an hour's moderate exercise every day, spending at least an hour a day practising relaxation and stress management techniques and following a low fat vegetarian diet, they can frequently help get rid of coronary artery blockages and heart pain. This advice is hardly likely to prove popular with surgeons and drug companies, of course. Sadly, I'm afraid that the potential for making money out of this sort of 'commonsense' regime is far too slight to please the medical establishment. If your doctor hasn't heard of the non-surgical, non-drug treatment of heart disease it is probably because she obtains all her post-graduate medical information from drug company sponsored lectures and publications.

Dr Ornish isn't the only doctor to have produced important work in this area. In a review entitled 'The Natural Cure of Coronary Heart Disease' (published in the journal *Nutrition and Health* in 2003, Dr Allan Withnell concluded that the medical literature: 'strongly suggests that lifestyle and particularly diet are the cause and the cure of coronary heart disease. The proof will lie in persuading the cardiac patient to change his lifestyle to the extent recommended and observing the result.' Dr Withnell has put emphasis on the words 'to the extent recommended' and his point is important. It's no good just cutting down from two burgers a day to one.

Naturally, patients with heart disease must get a doctor's advice and support before following this sort of regime. And it is, of course, vitally important that patients who are already taking drugs do not suddenly stop them (stopping drugs too quickly can be extremely dangerous – many modern drugs are so powerful that they need to be tailed off gradually when the time has come to stop them).

But my advice to anyone suffering from heart disease is simple: before you agree to surgery or consent to starting on what may well be a long-term course of drug therapy, do ask your doctor if she will help you follow the sort of programme initiated by Dr Ornish. If your doctor hasn't heard of this type of therapy for heart disease and isn't interested in finding out more then I suggest that you find another medical adviser. Any medical practitioner who is so wedded to drug company propaganda that she won't even consider this type of minimalist interventionist therapy isn't worth patronising.

And even if this holistic approach to heart disease does not completely remove all your symptoms (and, according to the evidence the odds are very much in your favour that it will) the chances are high that you will become much healthier and stronger. You will, therefore, be better able to cope with the traumas of whatever surgery or drug therapy you might need.

\* \* \*

There is, surely, sound advice in this philosophy for those who are fortunate enough not to be suffering from heart disease.

If learning to relax, taking gentle, regular exercise and eating a low fat vegetarian diet can help reverse existing heart disease then I believe it must be true that the same sort of regime will almost certainly help prevent heart disease. I know it isn't fashionable or exciting to offer simple advice but I'm more interested in offering accurate, honest, effective advice than in offering you an exciting sounding remedy that no one has ever heard of and which you can only buy after visiting dozens of stores. My aim is to help you live a long and healthy life – not to impress you by advising you to take a handful of rare Guatemalan beans and a couple of highly coloured and untested chemical cocktail pills every day.

The key to my simple advice for a healthy heart, is that it must be followed enthusiastically and regularly. Going for a walk once a fortnight, eating slightly less butter and making a half-hearted attempt to relax when you can feel your muscles knotting up is not going to make any noticeable difference at all.

In my view, assuming that you are in good health and there are no medical reasons why you should not do any of them, you should, if you want to make a difference, do several things in order to maintain good cardiac condition.

First, you should go for a brisk walk three times a week for around half an hour at a time. Don't be put off just because it's windy or because you are busy.

Second, you should make a serious attempt to cut down your consumption of fatty foods. Here, for example, are some quick ways to reduce the fat in your diet:

1.  Become vegetarian or vegan. Most meat is rich in fat. Fatty beef and pork are really bad for you but even chicken contains far too much fat for a low fat diet.

2.  Grill, steam, casserole, bake or boil but don't fry or roast food. (Stir-frying is OK.)

3.  Avoid butter, cream, margarine and full cream milk. Choose soya milk instead of dairy milk. Add herbs instead of butter (or salt) when cooking vegetables. Select low fat non-dairy spreads which contain polyunsaturated fats rather than saturated fats.

4.  If you buy prepared or convenience foods make sure that you look for low fat labels. Check food constituents and remember that you are aiming at a diet which contains less than 20 per cent fat. (The recommended figure is 10 per cent). Try to put products back onto the shelf if the label tells you that they contain more than 20 per cent fat. (In my view recommended 'acceptable' levels,

which are sometimes 30 per cent, are far too high.)

You should make a real effort to reduce your exposure to unnecessary stress. The simple way to do this is to make a list of all the activities and commitments in your life which contribute to your general stress levels and to then ask yourself which of those activities and commitments add value to your life and which can be avoided or discarded.

And finally, you should learn how to relax your mind and your body and you should practise what you learn on a regular basis. (There is advice about mental and physical relaxation in my books *Bodypower* and *Mindpower*).

## 18 | Learn To Listen To Your Body

Your body can tell you a lot if you will listen to it. Many minor symptoms which you might regard as a nuisance, or which you might hurry to treat, are early signs that something is wrong. Other signs may be ignored because you are not aware of their importance.

Here are some pointers to help you listen to your body more attentively.

1. If you are lifting or moving something and you feel a twinge of pain, consider that a warning. If you persist then you are probably going to end up with a strained muscle or damaged joint. If you are digging the garden and your back begins to ache that is an early sign that you would be foolish to ignore. Most episodes of pain should be regarded as early warning signs – the longer you ignore a pain the more likely you are to end up with a serious problem.

2. Vomiting and diarrhoea may be extremely inconvenient but they are sometimes important defence mechanisms employed by your body for very specific purposes. If you develop either of these symptoms without any other signs there is a chance that you may have acquired some form of gastrointestinal infection and that your body is trying to get rid of the infection. Any treatment you choose to employ to control your symptoms may also ensure that the infection stays in your body for longer. You must always consult your doctor immediately about either of these symptoms.

3. The cough reflex is a sophisticated defence system designed to eject unwelcome foreign matter from your respiratory tract. You should help your body by spitting out anything that you cough up. If you have a persistent or recurrent cough then you could have a

persistent or recurrent infection or irritation in your lungs. Or there could be an irritant of some kind in the air you breathe. If you have a cough it isn't always sensible to try to stop it – the cough is, after all, trying to protect your body. The best solution is to enlist your doctor's help and find the cause of the cough.

4. If you develop an unusual or unexpected skin rash the chances are high that you have been in contact with an irritant. The reaction of your skin is a result of the fact that your skin tissues, recognising the irritant as a threat, have produced chemicals designed to counteract it. You can probably ease the resultant rash by using powerful drug therapy to oppose your body's reaction. But it is far more sensible to identify the irritant and avoid it.

5. If you develop cramp in your legs it may be because your circulation has been impeded. The cramp pains develop because the waste products from the metabolic processes which occur during muscle use have accumulated. The slowing down of the circulation has meant that the blood has not been able to clear the wastes away. The cramp pains tell you to change position. Once you have acted the blood will flow more easily. The waste products can then be washed away, and the pain will disappear.

6. If you eat the wrong sort of food, or eat too quickly, you may develop indigestion. If you do, your stomach will be telling you that you have done something wrong. You can solve the problem temporarily by using antacids or by taking tablets. Do that, however, and the pain will probably come back. To get rid of the symptoms permanently you must listen to your body and take notice. Maybe you need to change your diet. Maybe you need to change your eating habits. You probably need good medical advice.

7. If you have a lot of accidents, it may be that you are constantly under too much pressure. There is a strong correlation between accident proneness and stress.

8. A woman who has irregular menstrual periods may well be worried about something. Girls who are taking examinations often have delayed periods – and so do girls who think they may be pregnant.

9. Most headaches are caused by pressure, tension and anxiety producing tight and tense muscles. Relaxing those muscles will

often help a tension headache disappear more speedily than taking a pill. Relaxing the muscles at an early stage, and dealing with the underlying tension, may stop a headache developing. Persistent, recurrent or worrying headaches should always be investigated by a doctor.

10. Blood pressure often rises as a result of stress. Taxi drivers, school teachers and surgeons are far more likely to develop high blood pressure than accountants, church ministers or farmers. If your doctor tells you that you have high blood pressure the chances are high that stress is damaging your health. You can help yourself by exposing yourself to less stress or by improving your resistance to stress.

You will find more about how to listen to your body in my book *Bodypower*. Remember that you should always seek professional medical advice for any symptoms which persist for more than five days, which reappear or which worry you.

# 19   LEARN TO CONTROL PAIN WITHOUT YOUR DOCTOR

Pain is the most common reason why people seek medical advice. It is the most important reason why people take pills. It causes more misery than all other symptoms put together. It ruins lives and wrecks careers.

And yet many doctors aren't very good at all at dealing with pain. Experts claim that up to three quarters of all patients with persistent pain get poor treatment.

There are, I believe, two main reasons for this. First, medical schools spend far too little time teaching students about ways to deal with pain. Many standard medical textbooks don't even mention pain. Second, the education of doctors is largely controlled by the drugs industry which has a vested interest in selling new, expensive and profitable products.

So, here is a quick summary of some of the things you really need to know about pain control techniques. You should only use these techniques with your doctor's approval. Never treat pain without obtaining medical advice. If your doctor hasn't heard of any of these techniques (and a surprising number of doctors still haven't heard of TENS machines, for example) ask him or her to do a little research and then give you his or her opinion.

## Drugs

Drugs are the commonest way of dealing with pain. There are scores of different products for doctors to choose from when writing out prescriptions for painkillers. And there are scores of products that you can buy without a prescription. But although painkillers can be extremely effective they aren't always used properly. You should always take painkillers according to the recommended instructions.

## TENS machines

There seems to me to be a conspiracy between doctors and drug companies which ensures that millions of patients in pain are denied easy, cheap, reliable pain relief so that drug company profits can remain high.

When body tissues are damaged messages carrying information about the injury travel towards the brain along two quite separate sets of nerve fibres. The larger fibres carry messages about sensations other than pain and the smaller fibres carry the pain messages. The messages which travel along the larger fibres tend to arrive at the spinal cord before the messages travelling along the smaller fibres and, if there are enough non-painful sensations travelling, the pain messages won't be able to get through. When you rub a sore spot you are increasing the number of non-pain messages travelling towards your brain – and thereby blocking the pain.

Once scientists had realised just how rubbing a sore or painful place can relieve pain the next step was to come up with a way of stimulating the passage of non-painful sensations even more efficiently.

The knowledge that all nerves within an inch or so of the surface of the skin can be stimulated by electrodes which are simply stuck onto the skin, encouraged medical researchers to give patients pocket sized battery operated stimulators which sent out a continuous series of electrical pulses. The pulses got into the large nerves of the body via silicon electrodes stuck onto the skin with a special conducting paste. And the electrical pulses – non-pain messages – stopped the pain messages getting through.

More exciting still it was found that Transcutaneous Electrical Nerve Stimulation (it quickly became known as TENS) did not just stimulate the passage of sensory impulses designed to inhibit the passage of pain impulses; it also stimulated the body to start producing its own pain-relieving hormones: the endorphins.

TENS machines are convenient, safe and effective. They are also cheap to buy and cheap to run.

In a study conducted with patients suffering from rheumatoid arthritis it was found that TENS equipment produced pain relief in up to 95 per cent of patients with up to 50 per cent of patients getting long-term relief.

But it isn't just arthritis patients who benefit from using TENS machines. TENS machines have been shown to be effective in the treatment of all kinds of pain.

With this sort of success available from a small, cheap, portable, long lasting machine that can be used at home without any training and that does not seem to produce any side effects at all, you might imagine that doctors would be recommending TENS machines to millions of patients – and that shops would have different models stocked high on their shelves.

But if you try to buy a TENS machine you'll have difficulty.

Why?

Cynics might suggest it is because drug companies don't want patients in pain to be able to deal with their symptom so easily and quickly and cheaply. Drug companies make huge amounts of money out of selling drugs to pain sufferers and TENS machines would cost them a fortune in lost sales.

Even governments (which try to do their best to keep the drug companies happy) are doing their best to stop people buying TENS machines.

You ought to be able to buy one in your chemist's shop. But I doubt if you'll be able to. If you want to try one ask your doctor or visit www.tenspen.com.

Now you will perhaps understand why I say that if a scientist found a cure for cancer or heart disease the drug industry – far more enthusiastic about continuing to sell vast quantities of useless pharmaceutical rubbish than in curing people – would suppress it.

### The rocking chair

One of the most effective ways of managing persistent, long-term backache that doctors can't cure is to sit in a rocking chair. Using a rocking chair stimulates the production of nerve impulses which provide effective and continuous pain relief. Since pain tends to get worse in the evening it may be a good idea to sit in your rocking chair while relaxing and watching TV.

### Heat

Heat can help just about any type of pain – but it can work best on the sort of pain produced by bruises, strains and inflamed joints. To apply heat to specific areas of your body try heated towels, an electrically heated pad, a sun lamp or a good old-fashioned hot water bottle.

If you use a hot water bottle make sure that the rubber is not perished, that the stopper fits well and that the bottle is wrapped in a towel so that it doesn't burn you.

## Ice

Pain experts have shown that ice can relieve headache pain in 80 per cent of patients and can relieve toothache in over 50 per cent of cases. It's also good for bruises, joint pain and backache. With your doctor's approval put crushed ice into a hot water bottle or wrap ice cubes in a thin towel. Don't hold ice on your skin for more than five minutes and remove it as soon as the area feels numb.

## Music

Four thousand years ago Hindu doctors used to play soothing, gentle music while surgeons were operating. And they used to have musicians playing in the wards too. They discovered that music helped people relax and banished pain. Recently, researchers in Warsaw have shown that music therapy is excellent at relieving pain. You'll have to experiment to find the type of music that helps you most. You may find that a portable cassette player with a pair of headphones is useful.

## 20 | BE CAREFUL WHEN BUYING MEDICINES OVER THE COUNTER

Selling medicines over the counter, without a prescription, is big business.

However, my advice is that you should think very carefully before spending huge amounts of money on buying medicines over the counter. Many of the products which are on sale in thousands of outlets everywhere have never been proven to be effective or useful and some of the products on sale can undoubtedly be dangerous.

Apart from the risk of side effects the other big problem you face when you take over-the-counter medicines is that you may have made the wrong diagnosis – and you may miss a serious underlying disorder.

For example, if you have persistent indigestion and you keep taking an anti-indigestion remedy there is a risk that in due course you could develop an ulcer – which could bleed and even kill you. Visit your doctor with persistent symptoms of indigestion and he will, hopefully, want to investigate.

If you have persistent diarrhoea and you keep buying a medicine to stop this symptom you may be missing an early sign of bowel cancer.

If you have a persistent cough and you keep buying bottles of cough medicine you could miss a serious chest problem which your doctor might have diagnosed early if you had visited him soon enough.

My general rule is that in order to minimise the risk of missing something serious you should not take a medicine you have bought yourself for any problem which continues for five days or more, or for any problem which recurs. Nor should you buy an over-the-counter medicine if you are already taking a prescribed drug. And, if you are in any doubt about the diagnosis and the treatment, you should get medical advice.

Home medicines – drugs that you have bought over the counter – can be handy and they can save unnecessary visits to the doctor. And if you have a good relationship with a pharmacist whom you trust then there is no doubt that you can benefit. But do bear in mind that the majority of symptoms which can be cleared up with the aid of medicines bought over the counter will probably also clear up without any remedy.

## 21   How To Get The Best Out Of Your Doctor

Every week thousands of people put off going for a medical examination because they're too anxious or shy. But putting off a visit to the doctor because you're suffering from "pre-examination nerves" could be dangerous. So, here's my advice (aimed particularly at those who feel nervous or embarrassed when they know they have got to go and see a doctor) on how to get the best out of a visit to the doctor.

1.  Don't delay. If you have a problem which is worrying you make an appointment straight away – and make sure that you see your doctor as soon as possible. The longer you wait the more you'll worry – and the worse things could get.

2.  Be prepared for a physical examination. Would you be happy if a car mechanic tried to repair your car engine without lifting the bonnet? Dress in clothes you can get in and out of quickly. Stockings are usually easier than tights. Zips are quicker than buttons. Don't wear underwear that is going to embarrass you.

3.  Don't worry about embarrassing or shocking your doctor. There is nothing you can tell your doctor that will shock him. Every week thousands of women who have 'trouble down below' walk in to the surgery, complain of a minor skin rash or a swollen vein and walk out without saying what is really on their minds.

4.  Make up your mind beforehand what you want to tell your doctor. Write down a list of your important signs, symptoms, complaints and worries. Women who have not yet gone through the menopause should take along details of their last few periods.

5.  Don't be startled or offended by questions your doctor asks. If you

have a discharge your doctor will want to know how long you've had it and what it looks like. If you have a gynaecological or urological problem questions about your sex life are routine.

6. Decide beforehand what questions you want to ask your doctor – and what you want him to do. And remember that it is part of your doctor's job to explain things to you. If you've seen a hospital doctor and haven't understood what he's said ask your own family doctor to interpret the medical jargon for you.

7. Your doctor will write down what you tell him. It makes sense for you to write down everything that he tells you – particularly if he is giving you advice or instructions.

8. If at the end of the consultation you aren't happy then ask for a second opinion. If your own doctor refuses point blank to refer you for a second opinion then I suggest that you change doctors.

## 22 LEARN WHEN TO USE ALTERNATIVE MEDICINE

Is alternative medicine safe? Does it work?

Here are some brief notes on some of the best known forms of alternative medicine. But remember: if you are thinking of trying any form of alternative medicine then my advice is that you should check with your own doctor first. Make sure that he is happy about what you are planning to do. And do make sure that the alternative practitioner you intend to consult is properly trained.

These notes are not complete – they are merely intended to provide a very brief, personal introduction to a massive subject.

\* \* \*

**Acupressure**

Acupuncture with fingers rather than needles. Like acupuncture the idea is to stimulate the flow of energy along the body's natural channels. Acupressure is a cross between acupuncture and massage said to be very good for dealing with headaches, backache, muscle pains etc.

**Acupuncture**

The Chinese, who invented acupuncture, believe that the human body contains 12 channels along which internal energies flow. When one of these channels is blocked illness develops. Acupuncturists stick needles into the skin in an attempt to unblock the channels and allow the energy flow to continue. Over 1000 acupuncture points have now been identified. Acupuncture does work – particularly in the treatment of pain and it is recommended by the World Health Organisation. In addition to helping patients with pain it also works in the treatment of many other disorders.

## Alexander Technique
Founded at the turn of the last century by an Australian actor called F.M. Alexander who believed that many illnesses develop because we don't sit, stand or walk properly. People who've been trained in the Alexander technique claim it helps relieve many health problems – particularly bone and joint troubles, backache and stress disorders.

## Aromatherapy
Aromatherapists claim that by massaging patients with sweet smelling oils they can treat an enormous range of physical and mental disorders. They choose scented oils from specific flowers, plants and trees to influence moods and treat diseases. The massage itself may be soothing and relaxing.

## Chiropractic
Chiropractic was established by a Canadian called Daniel Palmer who believed that 95 per cent of illnesses are caused by displaced bones in the spine – and can, therefore, be cured by manipulating the spine. There is evidence available to suggest that chiropractic can be useful in the treatment of bone and joint disorders – for example backache.

## Healing
There are thousands of healers in practice. Healers work in many different ways. Some lay their hands on their patients. Some say they don't need to touch their patient. Many work free of charge. There's evidence to show that healers can produce 'miraculous' results. No one really knows whether this is because they trigger off the body's self-healing powers or because of mysterious forces. There are virtually no risks or side effects with healing.

## Herbalism
One of the oldest branches of medicine. Many modern drugs are derived from herbal remedies. Drug companies base much of their research on looking for useful compounds that can be prepared from plants. About a third of the drugs doctors prescribe are plant-based. Today many millions of people have turned away from orthodox medicine and prefer to use herbal remedies. Herbal remedies are available for just about every illness imaginable.

There is no doubt that many herbal remedies do work – whether bought over the counter or prescribed by a herbalist.

## Homeopathy

Modern homeopathy was invented by Samuel Hahnemann in the 19th century. He believed that he could cure patients with minute doses of drugs. The theory is that the incredibly small doses trigger off the body's self-healing mechanisms. Homeopathy has much in common with vaccination in which a small amount of a foreign substance is introduced into the patient's body in order to stimulate the body's defence mechanisms. It really does seem to work.

## Hypnotherapy

Modern hypnotherapy began with Franz Mesmer in Vienna in the 18th century. When used by a skilled expert it can be useful and effective. There's evidence to show that hypnotherapy can help patients relax and deal with stress.

## Hydrotherapy

Simply means treatment using water. Hydrotherapy is practised in many health farms and alternative clinics. You can sit in it, be sprayed with it or drink it. You can have it very cold or very hot. Those who believe in hydrotherapy claim it can be used to treat all sorts of illnesses.

## Music therapy

Four thousand years ago Hindu doctors used to play soothing music while surgeons operated. They used to have music played in the wards too – they believed it helped patients get better. They may have been right. The value of music therapy seems clear. Music helps cure emotional and mental problems – and helps relieve pain.

## Meditation

Many modern diseases are caused by stress – and by our inability to relax. Meditation is a relaxation technique which works – and which can be easily learned for home use. My book *Mindpower* contains more information.

**Naturopathy**

Naturopathy was founded by Hippocrates around 400 BC who said that the best way to maintain good health was to eat and exercise moderately and carefully. Simple naturopathy means having a healthy lifestyle.

**Osteopathy**

Founded in 1874 by Andrew Tayler Still, an American who believed that the faults in the bony part of the body cause many diseases. Osteopaths claim that they can treat illnesses by manipulating the body – especially the spine. I don't think there is much difference between chiropractic and osteopathy. Excellent for problems such as backache. Some experts say that half of the patients going to an osteopath have backache. Many doctors with back trouble seek help from osteopaths.

*Five reasons why alternative medicine may be useful*

1.  Alternative remedies are often more 'natural' than orthodox medical remedies – they allow and encourage the body to heal itself.

2.  It is often possible to learn alternative techniques for home use – gaining independence from professionals.

3.  Most – but not all – forms of alternative medicine are relatively safe. The risk of side effects are usually low.

4.  Alternative practitioners are not usually as rushed as orthodox doctors – they have more time to talk to patients.

5.  There are not usually any waiting lists for alternative treatment.

## 23 IMPROVE YOUR HEALTH SIMPLY BY CHANGING YOUR DIET

Many patients who seek medical help could get better simply by changing their diet. And many more could have avoided illness altogether if they had been more careful about what they had eaten. The food you choose to eat can keep you fit, strong and healthy. Or it can make you ill. The list of diseases associated with food seems to get longer every year.

To help you eat healthily I've prepared a list of just some of the disorders known to be linked to particular eating habits. You could notice a genuine improvement in your condition – or help stop an existing problem getting worse – by selecting your diet with care.

One word of warning. Do have a word with your doctor if you are receiving any medical treatment and you plan to change your diet. Your need for medication may vary if your change of diet improves your health.

### Allergies

Hay fever and eczema are often caused by allergies. Eczema affected 2 people per 1000 born in 1946 but over 12 per 1000 of the following generation. Junk food may be one factor. Eat less additive rich food, less highly refined food and more fresh fruit and vegetables. But avoid GM (genetically modified) food. I have an as yet unsubstantiated hunch that the increase in hayfever sufferers may be linked to the growth in GM crops. My own hayfever, which had more or less disappeared, has reappeared recently suggesting that a new allergen – possibly pollen from GM crops – is responsible. There is no evidence that GM foods are dangerous because no one has done any clinical trials. To say that

GM foods are 'safe' is as logical as claiming that beating people over the head with sticks is safe simply because there is no scientific evidence proving that it is dangerous.

### Anaemia
You need iron to avoid anaemia. But you don't have to eat lots of fat rich meat to get the iron you need. Green vegetables and beans contain iron, and eating fresh fruit and vegetables will help your body absorb iron more effectively.

### Anxiety
Cut down your caffeine intake and reduce the amount of sugar in your diet.

### Asthma
Try to eat less dairy produce – milk, butter and cheese. And cut down on fatty meat. Eat more vegetables, fruit and nuts.

### Cancer
Between one third and one half of all cancers are linked to food. Eat less fat, avoid meat and eat more fruit, more vegetables and more wholegrain cereals.

### Constipation
Eat plenty of fibre and roughage.

### Diabetes
Cut down on sugar and fat but eat more fibre.

### Gall bladder disease
Eat less fatty food. Increase your intake of fibre rich fruit, vegetables and whole grain cereals.

### Gout
To avoid or control gout you should restrict your intake of alcohol and reduce the amount of meat you eat. Also limit your intake of fish, peas and beans.

## Headaches

To cut down your risk of suffering from headaches eat less chocolate, alcohol, fatty food and additive rich food. Cut down on caffeine too.

## Heart disease

Cut down the amount of fat you eat. Butter, milk, cream, fatty cheese and fatty meat should all be kept to a minimum.

## High blood pressure

Cut down your intake of salt by reducing your consumption of processed foods, canned foods, junk food, crisps, salted peanuts, salted cheese or butter, sausages, bacon and table salt.

## Indigestion

Avoid fried and fatty foods.

## Irritable bowel syndrome

Avoid fats and cut down dairy produce.

## Premenstrual syndrome

Reduce your intake of caffeine, milk, sugar and salt.

## Rheumatoid arthritis

Eat a low fat diet. And cut out meat.

You can find out more about the way the food you eat affects your health by reading my book *Food for Thought*.

## 24 How To Cut Your Cancer Risk By 80 Per cent

Doctors spend enormous amounts of time, energy and money on treating cancer but don't spend much time telling their patients how to *avoid* cancer

However, astonishingly, doctors now know what causes 80 per cent of all cancers. It is my view that you should be able to reduce your cancer risk by 80 per cent by avoiding those 'triggers' which are known to be responsible for causing cancer.

Here is my advice:

1. Don't smoke tobacco and keep away from other people who smoke tobacco.
2. Cut your consumption of fatty food.
3. Do not eat meat.
4. Eat plenty of fresh fruit and vegetables.
5. Eat plenty of fibre and whole grain foods.
6. Do not have any unnecessary X-rays.
7. Do not spend long periods of time in the sun.
8. Try not to live underneath or close to electricity power lines or close to an electricity supply station. Do not sleep or sit too close to electrical appliances.
9. Avoid foods which contain large quantities of additives.
10. Keep your weight under control.
11. Minimise your consumption of alcohol.
12. Avoid smoked, salt-cured, salt-pickled or barbecued foods.

## 25 │ NEVER EAT ANOTHER MEAL AND STAY SLIM AND HEALTHY FOR LIFE

Few single factors affect your health – and your life expectancy more than your weight. If you want to live a long, healthy life then you need to be thin. Forget all that nonsense about chubby people being happy and healthy. Fat folk may be happy. But not for long. Important research – which involved following over 100,000 women for more than a decade – has found that many cancer deaths and more than half of all cardiovascular deaths are due to excess weight. Even if you are just moderately overweight your health is at risk.

Women who are thirty per cent above their ideal weight are four times as likely to die of heart disease and twice as likely to die of cancer as are slimmer women. Women who are overweight seem more likely to die of cancer of the colon, breast and endometrium. And similar figures probably apply to men too. If you weigh just 22 pounds more than you did when you were 18-years-old then you are probably at risk.

So, the choice is yours. Being fat doesn't just mean not being able to wear fashionable clothes. It means dying sooner too.

Despite the importance of losing excess weight for good health doctors really are not very good at helping people slim successfully.

Instead of teaching patients sensible eating habits doctors have a terrible tendency to try and produce a 'miracle cure'. It has, for example, been popular for many doctors to prescribe amphetamine slimming pills (which can be addictive) or to recommend surgery as a remedy for obesity.

Every year thousands of people who want to lose weight risk their health and their lives having operations that will, at best, result in a small and temporary weight loss but which may, too often, result in either a lifetime of agony or an early death.

Ever since a surgeon earned himself a fortune in 19th century England by removing thousands of yards of intestine from his corpulent patients surgeons have been enthusiastically offering immediate 'magic' answers to patients wanting to lose weight without having to go through the alleged agonies of dieting.

All operations are potentially hazardous. Once a surgeon sticks a knife into you there are risks that things will go wrong. If the operation you're having is going to save your life then the risks are worth taking. But operations performed on slimmers aren't usually life-saving procedures – and I do not think that the risks are ever worth taking.

In my view there are dozens of safe and effective ways for people to lose weight but surgery is not one of them. I believe that using surgery to tackle obesity is like using a nuclear bomb to tackle an unruly soccer crowd – it is a totally inappropriate use of modern skills and technology. (For advice on how to lose weight safely and permanently see my book *Food for Thought*.)

## 26 Stay Healthy By Hugging, Kissing And Cuddling

The chances are high that you touch and cuddle the people you love far too little.

Touching – and being touched – is good for everyone. Hugging and cuddling the people you love can help protect you (and them) from disease.

If small children aren't touched often they quickly become seriously depressed. They may stop eating and simply fade away. It's not unknown for a child to die of love starvation. Even when things don't get that bad children often suffer lasting damage if they aren't touched and cuddled frequently. Children who are deprived of physical love often grow up to be promiscuous – unable to settle down with one partner as they are driven on in an endless search for more and more love.

And it isn't only children who suffer if they're deprived of hugs and cuddles. Without regular signs of physical affection we all become brittle, unstable and more susceptible to stress and pressure.

Ask yourself how many times you've hugged the people who are closest to you in the last 24 hours. And ask yourself how often you've touched the people you love.

If you don't touch or hug or cuddle people often it may be that you have to battle against a feeling that such outward signs of affection are wrong.

If your parents didn't hug or cuddle you very often you may find it difficult to let yourself go. You may have even been encouraged to believe that hugging, cuddling and touching are embarrassing or too 'showy'.

Boys are often told off for wanting a hug.

'You're too old for that sort of thing,' a man will say to his son, because he feels uncomfortable at the prospect of close physical contact.

If you think that you need to touch – and be touched – more often then make today the day you start.

♦ When you greet a loved one – even if it is only after a parting of a few hours – put an arm around them. You don't have to start with a full blooded hug if that makes you feel embarrassed. Build up to a hug slowly. When you greet close friends get into the habit of touching them – maybe clasping their hands or touching their forearm, or perhaps putting an arm around them.

♦ When you're leaving someone – again if it's only for a few hours – touch them on the arm or shoulder. Again, build up to a proper cuddle.

♦ Don't let children fool you when they wriggle away if you're trying to hug them. All children like to receive physical signs of affection (though they may be embarrassed about it in public – especially if other children's parents don't show any signs of affection). Wait until you're somewhere private to show how you feel.

♦ When you kiss someone 'hello' or 'goodbye' don't be content with a distant peck on the cheek. Put your arms around them and give them a big hug too.

Hugging, touching and kissing aren't just for lovers. If you regularly hug, touch and kiss all the people who matter to you then you'll feel better – and so will they.

## 27 IN NINE OUT OF TEN ILLNESSES YOUR BODY WILL HEAL ITSELF

Many of the people who are injured by doctors never needed medical treatment in the first place.

The human body contains a comprehensive variety of self-healing mechanisms which mean that in nine out of ten illnesses your body will mend itself.

It is important that you learn to understand your body; learn to appreciate your own self-healing skills; learn to acknowledge your body's miraculous range of techniques for dealing with threats and diseases; and learn to know when your body can look after itself − and when you need professional help.

The big trouble with most health care professionals − and this includes acupuncturists, osteopaths, aromatherapists and all other 'alternative' practitioners, as well as orthodox doctors − is that they tend to treat their patients as battle grounds, the illness as an enemy and their own armoury of drugs or techniques as weapons with which to fight the illness.

Whether he sticks needles into you, gives you herbal tea to drink or prescribes a drug for you to swallow the therapist has to do something to you, or give you something to take, in order to justify his fee.

The evidence to show that this interventionist philosophy is wrong is incontrovertible. When you fall ill you do not necessarily need to have anything done to you. Your body is equipped with such an enormous range of subtle and sophisticated feedback mechanisms that it can look after itself very well.

Your body can heal itself, protect itself and guard itself against a thousand different types of threat.

Your body contains internal mechanisms designed to enable you to deal automatically with minor damage, improve your eyesight, keep out the cold, deal with anxiety and even help fight against diseases as threatening as cancer.

Your internal appetite control centre can ensure that you eat only the foods that your body needs – and it can help make sure that you never become overweight.

Your body's internal pain relieving hormones are as powerful as morphine – but you have to know how to take advantage of those pain relieving hormones.

The human brain even contains a natural drug designed to help anxiety.

Your body is marvellous. It contains a vast variety of extraordinarily effective self-healing mechanisms. Most of them you probably don't even know about. And if you don't know about them then you probably don't know how to take advantage of them.

Your body cannot always cope, of course.

There will be times when even your sophisticated self-healing mechanisms will be overwhelmed and will need support.

But to dismiss these mechanisms on the grounds that they don't provide a complete answer to all health problems is like arguing that it isn't worthwhile learning to swim because occasionally you may need the help of a lifeguard.

I firmly believe that if you learn to use the power of your own body you will benefit in a number of ways.

First, of course, you will reduce the risk of being injured by a healthcare professional. Every year thousands of people suffer because of treatments used by orthodox and alternative practitioners.

Second, you will benefit because when an interventionist treats an illness he usually tries to oppose your body's own internal responses, as well as whatever outside agent may have triggered those responses in the first place. This isn't necessarily a good idea. All symptoms are merely signs that a fight is taking place inside your body. Unless the interventionist treatment is carefully designed to support and aid the fight the treatment applied may well end up damaging and even weakening your body's internal mechanisms – eventually making you more vulnerable and more reliant on interventionists and their treatments.

It is vitally important that you learn to use your body's powers and learn to recognise precisely when you need professional support. You should retain overall control of your body and bring in the healers as advisers and technicians.

Once you've mastered the idea of using your body's own healing powers you will find yourself enjoying a freedom that you might otherwise never know.

I have described the many wonderful ways in which your body can look after itself in my book called *Bodypower*. The book explains how you can use your body's self-healing powers to help you deal with 9 out of 10 illnesses without a doctor – it has been described as an 'owner's manual' for a human body.

## 28 | How To Live To Be 100

Here are 50 tips which will (if you follow them) make a real difference to your life expectancy.

1. Don't lie in bed in the mornings. People who live to be 100 are invariably early risers.

2. Be careful not to eat too much. The type of food you eat is important. But the amount you eat is important too. Overeating puts a strain on your body – and leads to obesity, which is a real killer. Most of us eat far too much – especially in winter when rolls of fat are covered up by layers of thick clothes. Too much food will make you lethargic and tired. When you put food on your plate ask yourself if you really *need* that much. If the answer is 'no' then take less.

3. If you are feeling glum visit a local travel agent and come away with an armful of brochures. Just dreaming about wonderful holidays can help you relax and feel good.

4. Drink alcohol in moderation. A small amount of alcohol may improve your health. Too much alcohol will damage your health.

5. Do not dwell too much on the past. If you are constantly moaning that life was better in the 'good old days' then you will reduce your chances of having a long and healthy life. If you're going to live through ten decades then you must be adaptable – and prepared to cope with the fact that the world around you will constantly change.

6. Giving up work is often a signal for the body to slow down. If you intend to retire from work then make sure that you find something else to keep yourself busy.

7. Be as independent as you can be. Don't let other people push you

around or control your life. The more you can control your destiny the healthier you will be. Contrary to all the myths, bosses rarely suffer from as much stress as those who work for them.

8.  Take as few pills as you can. Constantly taking drugs (both those prescribed and those bought from the pharmacist) will damage your body.

9.  Try not to worry about your health. If you are constantly expecting to fall sick then you will fall sick. People who live long, healthy lives rarely worry about illness or death – they just get on with life.

10. Avoid dieting. Constantly gaining and losing weight will damage your body.

11. Do not smoke. And keep away from people who smoke. Breathing in other people's second-hand tobacco smoke can permanently damage your health.

12. Find a hobby you really enjoy – and throw yourself into it with enthusiasm. Choose something that you've always wanted to try. Enrol in night school classes or borrow a book from the library or join a correspondence course. A new hobby will put passion and excitement back into your life.

13. Avoid sugar rich foods.

14. Avoid fatty foods.

15. Eat plenty of fresh fruit and vegetables. And buy less stuff in packets. Spend ten minutes reading the packets in your food cupboard and you will probably be horrified to see how many chemicals you are eating. The average diet consists of a mixture of fat and chemicals.

16. Don't eat meat. Meat causes cancer. And your body doesn't need it.

17. Share your emotions with the people who are closest to you. Don't bottle-up your feelings. If you feel the need to cry – then cry. If you feel angry then shout.

18. Say 'I love you' at least once a day to the person you love most in the world. And make sure that they say 'I love you' to you. Those three words make us feel wanted. We live in a world that is too often cruel and thoughtless and full of anger and hatred. Knowing that someone loves you will help protect you against the toxic stress in your life.

19. Exercise at least three times a week – and preferably every day. The best forms of exercise are: walking, cycling, swimming and

dancing. Exercise should never hurt and should always be fun but if you don't need a bath or shower after exercising then you probably haven't exercised properly. (You should always check with your doctor before starting to exercise). If you join a gym make sure that you get expert advice from a qualified professional. Visit the local swimming pool. Make an effort to do something physical. It's too easy to slump down in front of the TV set. Your body needs regular work-outs. Without exercise you'll become stale, flaccid and vulnerable to germs. Make sure you take the right amount of exercise. Too much can be just as bad for you as too little. Three quarters of the population take too little exercise. Many of the remainder take too much. Exhaust yourself in the gym five nights a week and your battered and exhausted body will be exceptionally vulnerable to infection. I know many women and men who exhaust their bodies by leaping about at strenuous exercise classes. Too much exercise damages the immune system. You don't have to wear yourself out in the gym to keep in good shape. But you do need to take regular, fun exercise. Remember: check with your doctor before starting an exercise programme.

20. Spend half a day a week being selfish. Most of us try to cram too much sensible, useful living in to our lives. Spend half a day a week doing something that you enjoy. Go swimming. Go dancing. Go for a walk. Sit in the park. Indulge yourself. Have half a day a week that is all yours.

21. Drink plenty of fluids – particularly fresh water. Your kidneys need a good supply of water in order to function properly.

22. Eat a banana a day. Bananas are better for you than apples. They are packed with fibre and vitamins. But most important of all they come ready wrapped so that when you eat one you don't have to worry about it being contaminated with chemicals or bugs. As a bonus bananas contain relatively few calories – so won't make you fat.

23. Make sure you have plenty of fun in your life. Gloomy workaholics tend to die early. People who live lengthy, healthy lives tend to regard life as an adventure to be enjoyed. A sense of humour is important. Read books that make you laugh. Watch videos that you find truly entertaining. Keep a library of favourite books and videos that you know you can turn to when you're feeling

miserable. Try to find something to laugh at every day.

24. When you are worried about something ask yourself what the bottom line is – the worst that can happen. Once you know the worst you will be surprised at how many fears suddenly become less significant.

25. Stop wasting your life. Put the phone down on unsolicited, unwanted calls and shut the door on unsolicited salesmen. In a week you'll save hours – enough time to do something you really enjoy. Unsolicited salesmen – usually selling us things we don't want or need – waste hours. And because they're using up your life they're building up your stress.

26. Buy a telephone with an 'on-off' button. Or buy a telephone answering machine – and use it to take calls when you want to rest. How many times have you sat down to relax and been disturbed by the phone? How many times have social evenings been interrupted by irrelevant calls? We allow the phone to rule our lives – and we let it get away with rude behaviour that we would never tolerate from children.

27. Keep a diary. You don't have to fill pages with your innermost thoughts. Or record tedious, mundane daily happenings. But keeping a diary will help you plan your life more effectively – and therefore avoid many unnecessary and unexpected stresses. A diary will also give you a chance to let off steam in private.

28. Do something physical whenever you feel angry. Or frustrated. Or let down. Go for a walk. Beat a rug. Dig the garden. If you aren't fit enough or strong enough to go for a walk or beat a rug, go somewhere private and shout. Getting your anger out of your system will help protect you from stress.

29. If you normally go to bed at the same time every evening try staying up late at night occasionally – watch a movie, go out to a party or just invite friends round to talk.

30. Work out how many of your waking hours you spend doing things you want to do; and how many you spend doing things that other people want you to do. If you spend more than half your time doing things for other people make an effort to make more time for yourself.

31. If your house is dimly lit buy bigger light bulbs. Living in half dark rooms can be depressing. Put in a bigger bulb and you're

unlikely to notice much difference in your electricity bill but the extra light will make your life seem brighter.

32. Make plans so that you have things to look forward to every week. It doesn't have to be anything complicated or expensive. Plan to meet a friend, go for a walk or see a movie. And don't let yourself pull out at the last minute because you want to slump down in front of the television.

33. If you drink tea or coffee drink it fairly weak. Caffeine – found in tea and coffee – is a powerful drug.

34. Make a real effort to look after your appearance – even if the weather is lousy and you have nowhere to go. Wearing bright, cheerful clothes – and looking good – will improve the way you feel. Try to avoid clothes in dark colours.

35. Frustration, tension, anger and worry all lead to stiff, uncomfortable muscles. The result is usually headaches and other pains. Try massaging your temples with your fingertips every evening. You'll feel fresher if you gently massage the whole of your face with your fingertips.

36. Wear the flimsiest, sexiest and most outrageous underwear you can find – and afford. It may not do much towards keeping you warm but it'll make you feel good during the day.

37. Send silly postcards to your five best friends – for no reason at all. It'll make you feel better and it'll make them feel good too.

38. If you're feeling physically exhausted or mentally fed up spend half an hour in a warm bath with a good book or magazine.

39. Go through the TV listings magazines and pick out programmes that you know you'll enjoy. The joy of anticipation is never disappointing.

40. Try to be selective about your TV watching. The average man, woman and child watches three, four or five hours of television a day. Every day. What a waste of a life.

41. Try this simple exercise to calm your entire body: take a deep breath in ; suck in your tummy muscles to make your tummy as hard as it will go; count to five; let your muscles go limp; empty the air out of your lungs. Repeat this several times until you feel thoroughly relaxed.

42. Never underestimate the power of your mind. Your mind can make you ill but it can also make you well again.

43. Always remember that if you develop new symptoms while being treated for a health condition there is a good chance that the new symptoms are caused by the treatment you are receiving for your existing condition.

44. Try to keep out of communal showers. School and sports changing rooms – where sweaty people gather together to huff and puff their germs at one another – are great places for picking up illnesses. Community cleansing should be banned. My advice: wrap up well in warm clothes and go home to bathe or shower.

45. Learn to listen to your body. When I was the regular doctor on breakfast television in the early 1980s and told viewers to do this one woman wrote in to say that she couldn't listen to her body because she was deaf. But you don't need ears to listen to your body. You should listen to your body simply by increasing your awareness of it. Watch out for early symptoms and take whatever action your body tells you is appropriate.

46. Never hand over your health, your body and your life to doctors or other professionals. If you need to obtain professional help make sure that you retain control. Call in the experts for their technical skills but remember that you should always retain responsibility and authority. Whenever possible make sure that you know what they plan to do to you – and what the risks are – before they do it. Remember that your body's self-healing powers (what I call 'bodypower') can enable you to recover from nine out of ten illnesses without any outside help. But even when you do need professional help your 'bodypower' can still help you.

47. Do not be afraid to mix and match orthodox and alternative treatments – but make sure that everyone who is treating you knows about any other treatments you are trying.

48. Learn to adapt. Our world changes more rapidly than at any time in history. To survive you must expect change and be prepared to adapt.

49. Be prepared to say 'No' when saying 'Yes' will put you under unnecessary stress or make you feel resentful.

50. Breathe clean air as often as you can. And be aware that if you work in a building where the same air is constantly re-circulated (to save on heating costs) you will end up sharing the coughs and colds of everyone else in the building.

# 29 Simple Tips To Help You Manipulate Your Doctor

Doctors use their desks to establish their authority. They sit behind them and use them as barriers – to establish their superiority. I know of one doctor who used to shave the bottoms off the front legs of the chair in which his patients sat. Because they were constantly sliding forwards, patients always felt slightly uncomfortable – and never wanted to stay too long.

When you visit the surgery and your doctor waves you to a chair a couple of feet in front of his desk he is putting you in an exposed and vulnerable situation. He possesses the desk and is defended by its bulk. You sit alone with your personal space unprotected.

But, as I showed in my book *People Watching* it is very easy to reverse the situation and take control.

When you enter the surgery move the chair a few inches so that it is closer to the desk. Then sit down so that you can lean forwards and put your elbows on the desk. If there is a letter rack in front of you gently but firmly move it to one side. Put your hat, gloves, newspaper, shopping, handbag or notebook down on the desk.

If your doctor is leaning forwards to establish his territorial rights over his desk he will almost certainly respond by leaning backwards and abandoning his control of the desk. His response will be automatic. You will then be able to start your consultation in a much stronger position. You will be in charge of the consultation – a much safer position from which to seek advice.

## 30 | MAKE YOUR VOICE HEARD – YOU'LL FEEL BETTER

We live in a world where cruelty is honoured, where dishonesty is rewarded, where power is taken by the vicious and the brutal and where the inept, the incompetent and the uncaring prosper.

We live in a world where integrity is sneered at, where honesty is described as controversy, where passion is regarded as an embarrassment and where the truth is a dangerous commodity.

We are ruled by pompous authoritarians who cloak their petty ambitions and personal greed in stolen power and glory but accept no responsibility for justice; today, the million horsemen of the Apocalypse gallop ever onwards in malignant determination to destroy truth, honesty and compassion.

Morals and ethics have become abstract subjects for university debate, rather than guidelines for our behaviour. No one cares any more about what is right. No one cares about the poor, the meek, the gentle and the kind. No one cares about the innocent.

Our society cares only about what is regarded as proper and 'normal'. The joy of giving is an object of scorn and derision. Nobility and honour are freely bought and sold.

We have dirtied our land and polluted our air and our water. We live in a filth of our own making; a filth that gets worse each day and which contaminates our very lives.

We applaud and reward the fat businessmen who cheat the world's poor. We kneel before the representatives of evil and daily pledge our allegiance to witless, passionless mediocrity. We treat those with whom we share this planet with idle, rough, contempt. We use them for our own ends without a thought for their comfort, happiness or dignity.

And yet we claim to be innocents in all this corruption of the spirit. We blame an unseen 'them' for the horrors of our world. We blame 'them' for the cruelty, the viciousness and the misery. We live in comfort and contentment; slumped in front of the TV screen; deaf to the injustices which mark our world.

It is a slick trick we play on ourselves.

For we are them and they are we.

If you want to know the identity of the mysterious 'them' all you have to do is look in the mirror. We have built this society. It is our responsibility. We cannot escape from blame by keeping silent. The evil that is done is done on your account and if you stay silent it is done with your blessing.

Remember, then, that it is up to you to shout 'stop' when you have had enough of the wickedness around you.

If you want to change things campaign and protest and do not rest until your voice is heard. If you do nothing then you are just a silent part of the evil which is corrupting and destroying our world.

What have you done in the past to fight cruelty and injustice?

And, more important, what do you plan to do in the future?

* * *

Readers often ask me whether campaigning ever works.

The answer is yes – it often takes a long time but campaigning can work.

For example, I first started my campaign to warn doctors and patients about the dangers of overprescribing benzodiazepine tranquillisers back in 1973. For ten years the only thing the campaign produced was a fairly constant stream of personal abuse – much of it from doctors who were offended that anyone should dare question the medical establishment. Editors who supported my campaign were reminded that most doctors disagreed with me. Because of my constant campaigning about tranquillisers I was constantly in trouble. Numerous doctors publicly claimed that the benzodiazepines were perfectly safe – and that I was irresponsible to frighten the public with articles, books and broadcasts about these drugs.

By the early 1980s, after ten years of campaigning, a growing number of doctors agreed that I was right. Gradually, as the campaign grew many other journalists and broadcasters joined in the battle. Whereas I had originally been a lone voice – and therefore relatively easy to dismiss – those defending the widespread use of benzodiazepine tranquillisers and sleeping tablets found themselves on the defensive. In 1988, the government in Britain finally took action – admitting that they had done so because of my articles. A fifteen year campaign had been vindicated.

The benzodiazepine campaign was exhausting, expensive and time consuming but it was clear from this battle that you and I do have power; we can change things. But we must fight together. Doctors and politicians responded to the benzodiazepine campaign when the protests could no longer be ignored. The lesson is that we must be persistent and determined.

* * *

If you care about the world in which you live and want it to be a better, safer place for humans and animals then you must make your voice heard. Don't worry if people scoff or mock. Don't allow yourself to be put off by scorn, derision, undisguised contempt or a lack of support or encouragement from others.

Just remember that imaginative, thoughtful and creative individuals have always had a hard time. Look back in history and you will find countless examples of citizens who were harassed or persecuted simply because they dared to think for themselves – and tried to share their thoughts with others.

Our world has never welcomed the original, the challenging, the inspirational or the passionate and has always preferred the characterless to the thought-provoking.

Those who dare to speak out against the establishment have always been regarded as dangerous heretics. The iconoclast has never been a welcome figure in any age.

Confucius, the Chinese philosopher, was dismissed by his political masters and his books were burned. Those who didn't burn his books within 30 days were branded and condemned to forced labour. Two and a half thousand years later Confucius's influence was still considered so dangerous that Chairman Mao banned his works.

Described by the Delphic Oracle as the wisest man in the world Greek teacher Socrates was accused of corrupting the youth of Athens, arrested for being an evil-doer and 'a person showing curiosity, searching into things under the earth and above the heaven and teaching all this to others'. Socrates was condemned to death.

Dante, the Italian poet, was banished from Florence and condemned to be burnt at the stake if ever captured.

After they had failed to silence him with threats and bribes the Jewish authorities excommunicated Spinoza in Amsterdam because he refused to toe the party line, refused to think what other people told him he must think and insisted on maintaining his intellectual independence. He and his work were denounced as 'forged in Hell by a renegade Jew and the devil'.

Galileo, the seventeenth century Italian mathematician, astrologer and scientist got into terrible trouble with the all-powerful Church for daring to support Copernicus, who had had the temerity to claim that the planets revolved around the sun.

Aureolus Philippus Theophrastus Bombastus von Hohenheim (known to his chums as Paracelsus) made himself enemies all over Europe because he tried to revolutionise medicine in the sixteenth century. Paracelsus was the greatest influence on medical thinking since Hippocrates but the establishment regarded him as a troublemaker.

Ignaz Semmelweiss, the Austrian obstetrician who recognised that puerperal fever was caused by doctors' dirty habits was ostracised by the medical profession for daring to criticise practical procedures.

Henry David Thoreau, surely the kindest, wisest philosopher who has ever lived, was imprisoned for sticking to his ideals.

Original thinkers and people who do not fit neatly into the scheme of things have never gone down well. And nothing has changed. Today, incompetence and mediocrity thrive and are now subsidised, supported and encouraged by our increasingly bureaucratic and intrusive society. Schoolteachers and social workers encourage mediocrity because they themselves are mediocre. Talent frightens them witless. Among bureaucrats and administrators incompetence and mediocrity are esteemed virtues; these be-suited morons revere the banal and worship the bland.

The unusual or the eccentric attract scorn and ridicule. Politicians are frightened of anything new or challenging. They reject the innovative, the creative and the imaginative in favour of the accustomed, the comfortable and the ordinary. It is hardly surprising that the sensitive, the thoughtful, the imaginative and the caring find twentieth century life almost too painful to bear.

If you feel that something is wrong, and you feel passionately that something ought to be done about it, then stand up for your principles, shout and make your voice heard. There is a chance that some people will regard you as a lunatic. I have no doubt that many small-minded people will sneer and tell you that in trying to change the world and root out dishonesty, corruption and injustice you are tilting at windmills. But there is also a chance that your voice will be heard; that others will respond and that you will win your battle. And the benefits of victory surely far outweigh the insults of the insignificant. Only when you have found something you are prepared to die for will you really know what life is all about.

## 31 | ROOT-FILLED TEETH MAY BE A TIME BOMB

Do you have any root-filled teeth? If so – beware! They may be a time bomb – waiting to go off at some unknown time in the future.

It now seems that it is possible that root-filled teeth may cause any one of a number of serious diseases – including some of the commonest and most troublesome degenerative diseases – such as arthritis, heart disease, muscle problems and many other conditions.

It is even possible that a root-filled tooth could kill you.

Bugs trapped inside a root filled tooth may sit there for years – apparently doing no harm. But another disease – or a stressful incident putting pressure on the body's immune system – may trigger the bugs into action.

No one really knows just how dangerous root-filled teeth can be. Many dentists dismiss the idea of danger out of hand. Some claim that they can eradicate all bugs before root-filling a tooth.

I think this confidence is misplaced.

I believe there is a real risk.

I suspect that having a tooth root-filled could lead to future health problems.

And I also believe that if you have a serious, chronic problem and you have a root-filled tooth the two could be connected.

There's no easy answer to this problem.

But I can tell you that if I had a long standing, troublesome health problem and a root-filled tooth I would want my doctors and dentist to consider the possibility that the two could be linked. Removing the root-filled tooth might provide a 'miracle' solution.

And in future I will think very carefully indeed – and be very reluctant – before allowing my dentist to root-fill any of my teeth.

## 32  Ritalin: Child Abuse On Prescription?

Family doctors are these days frequently under pressure (usually from teachers and social workers who know nothing about drug therapy to prescribe the drug called Ritalin for children who are accused of behaving badly, reported as not doing well at school or 'diagnosed' as suffering from something called Attention Deficit Hyperactivity Disorder (known as ADHD).

For several decades now Ritalin, and other drugs, have been prescribed for children diagnosed as suffering from various types of brain dysfunction and hyperactivity. (Other psychostimulants which have, at one time or another, been regarded as competitors to Ritalin have included Dexedrine).

The first problem is that Attention Deficit Hyperactivity Disorder (and other variations on the hyperactivity theme) is a rather vague diagnosis which is often leapt upon by teachers, social workers and parents to excuse and explain any unacceptable or uncontrollable behaviour.

Parents of children whose behaviour is in any way regarded as different or unusual are often encouraged to believe that their child is suffering from a disease for two simple reasons. First, it is more socially acceptable to give a child a pseudoscientific label than to have to admit that he or she may simply be badly behaved.

Second, when a child has been given a label it is possible to offer a treatment. Commonly it will be one, such as a drug, which takes away responsibility and offers someone a profit.

ADHD (aka Attention Deficit Disorder, or ADD, hyperkinetic child syndrome, minimal brain damage, minimal brain dysfunction in children, minimal cerebral dysfunction and psycho-organic syndrome in children) is a remarkably non-specific disorder. (I am always suspicious of diseases which have lots of names. Diabetes is diabetes. A broken leg is a broken leg.)

The symptoms which characterise ADHD (or whatever else it's being known as) may include: a chronic history of a short attention span, distractibility, emotional lability, impulsivity, moderate to severe hyperactivity, minor neurological signs and abnormal EEG. Learning may or may not be impaired.

Read that rather nonsensical list of symptoms carefully and you'll find that just about any child alive could probably be described as suffering from ADHD.

What child isn't impulsive occasionally? What child doesn't cry and laugh (that's what emotional lability means)? What child cannot be distracted?

So, by this definition, Ritalin could be recommended for any child who seemed bored and restless or who exhibited unusual signs of intelligence or skill. Read the biographies of geniuses and you may wonder what we are doing to our current generation of most talented individuals.

'Is Ritalin a drug in search of a disease?' wrote one author, and it isn't difficult to see why.

* * *

Ritalin has been recommended as a treatment for functional behaviour problems since the 1960s. By 1966 the 'experts' had come up with a definition of the sort of child for whom Ritalin could usefully be prescribed.

Children suffering from Minimal Brain Dysfunction (MBD), the first syndrome for which Ritalin was recommended, were defined as: 'children of near average, average or above average general intelligence with certain learning or behavioural disabilities ranging from mild to severe, which are associated with deviations of function of the central nervous system. These deviations may manifest themselves by various combinations of impairment in perception, conceptualization, language, memory and control of attention, impulse or motor function'.

Other symptoms which children might exhibit and which could be ascribed to MBD included: being sweet and even-tempered, being cooperative and friendly, being gullible and easily led, being a light sleeper, being a heavy sleeper and so on and on.

Given that sort of list to work with I find it difficult, again, to think of a child who wouldn't (theoretically) benefit from Ritalin.

\* \* \*

The bottom line is that it has become easy for social workers and teachers to define any child who misbehaves or doesn't learn 'properly' as suffering from MBD or ADHD. It's a convenient diagnosis which excuses parents, teachers and social workers from responsibility or any sense of guilt. How can the parents or the teacher be accused of failing when the child is ill and needs drug therapy?

Commercially, Ritalin and MBD became a huge success. By 1975 around a million children in the USA were diagnosed as suffering from MBD. Half of these were being given drugs and half of those on drugs were on Ritalin.

(For the sake of completeness I should point out that Ritalin has not always been used exclusively in the treatment of badly behaved children. When Dr Andrew Malleson wrote his book *Need Your Doctor Be So Useless* in 1973 he reported that the CIBA Pharmaceutical Company had suggested to doctors the use of their habit forming drug Ritalin for 'environmental depression' caused by 'noise: a new social problem'.)

\* \* \*

Does Ritalin work?

Well, that's a bit of a stinker of a question and I apologise for asking it, particularly since I can't answer it.

Actually, I honestly don't think anyone else can answer it either. The drug company which is now responsible for Ritalin in the UK, admits that 'data on...efficacy of long-term use of Ritalin are not complete'.

With one in twenty children said to be suffering from MBD (or ADHD or ADD or XYZ or whatever else anyone wants to call it), with Ritalin having been on the market and used for this condition for over three decades, and with some experts saying that a million children a year are given Ritalin in the USA alone you might find this a trifle disappointing. Just how long does it take to find out whether or not a drug works? Am I being horribly cynical in suggesting that it might be against the drug company's interests to find out whether or not Ritalin really works? After all, if long-term studies found that

Ritalin didn't work a very profitable drug would, presumably, lose some of its appeal.

Some research has been done. One five year study of hyperactive children who were given Ritalin at Montreal Children's Hospital found that the children did not differ in the long-term from hyperactive children who were not given the drug. In Johannesburg a study of 14 children is said to have produced a response in only 2 children. One child showed some deterioration and another showed marked deterioration.

At least one investigator has reported that drugs like Ritalin may produce a deterioration in learning new skills at school and parents have reported that the symptoms of MBD (or whatever else anyone wants to call it) have miraculously disappeared during school holidays.

The picture is confused by the fact that there may be a short-term improvement in behaviour among children given Ritalin. But is this a real improvement? Or is the child simply drugged and therefore less likely to do anything which might upset parents, social workers or teachers?

A child taking Ritalin might be less disruptive and I can see that being popular in schools. But is the drug really helping the child? And should we give a child a powerful and potentially hazardous drug because it keeps him quiet?

There is evidence suggesting that children who are genuinely hyperactive may have been poisoned by food additives or by lead breathed in from air polluted by petrol fumes. If this is so then is giving another potentially toxic drug really the answer to this problem?

\* \* \*

The next problem is that I believe that Ritalin can reasonably be described as potentially toxic. Ritalin has been described as 'very safe' but for the record here is a list of some of the possible side effects which may be associated with Ritalin: nervousness, insomnia, decreased appetite, headache, drowsiness, dizziness, dyskinesia, blurring of vision, convulsions, muscle cramps, tics, Tourette's syndrome, toxic psychosis (some with visual and tactile hallucinations), transient depressed mood, abdominal pain, nausea, vomiting, dry mouth, tachycardia, palpitations, arrhythmias, changes in blood pressure and heart rate, angina pectoris, rash, pruritus, urticaria, fever, arthralgia, alopecia, thrombocytopenia purpura, exfoliative dermatitis, erythema multiforme, leucopenia, anaemia and minor retardation of growth during prolonged therapy in children.

Doctors who prescribe Ritalin, and who have the time and the inclination to read the warnings issued with the drug, will discover that Ritalin should not be given to patients suffering from marked anxiety, agitation or tension since it may aggravate these symptoms.

Ritalin is contraindicated in patients with tics, siblings with tics or a family history or diagnosis of Tourette's syndrome. It is also contraindicated in patients with severe angina pectoris, cardiac arrhythmias, glaucoma, thyrotoxicosis, or known sensitivity to methylphenidate and it should be used cautiously in patients with hypertension (blood pressure should be monitored at appropriate intervals).

Ritalin should not be used in children under six years of age, should not be used as treatment for severe depression of either exogenous or endogenous origin and may exacerbate symptoms of behavioural disturbance and thought disorder if given to psychotic children.

The company selling it claims that although available clinical evidence indicates that treatment with Ritalin during childhood does not increase the likelihood of addiction, chronic abuse of Ritalin can lead to marked tolerance and psychic dependence with varying degrees of abnormal behaviour.

Ritalin, it is warned, should be employed with caution in emotionally unstable patients, such as those with a history of drug dependence or alcoholism, because such patients may increase the dosage on their own initiative.

Ritalin should also be used with caution in patients with epilepsy since there may be an increase in seizure frequency.

And height and weight should be carefully monitored in children as prolonged therapy may result in growth retardation. (A child might lose several inches in possible height – though if treatment is stopped there is a generally a growth spurt). It is perhaps worth mentioning here my view that if a drug is powerful enough to retard growth it does not seem entirely unreasonable to suspect that the chances are high that it may be having other powerful effects upon and within the body.

Doctors are also warned that careful supervision is required during drug withdrawal, since depression as well as renewed overactivity can be unmasked. Long-term follow-up may be needed for some patients.

There have also been reports that children have committed suicide after drug withdrawal. And one study has shown that children who are treated with stimulants alone had higher arrest records and were more likely to be institutionalised.

Long-term use of Ritalin has been said to cause irritability and hyperactivity (these are, you may remember, the problems for which the drug is often prescribed). In a study published in *Psychiatric Research* and entitled 'Cortical Atrophy in Young Adults With A History of Hyperactivity', brain atrophy was reported in more than half of 24 adults treated with psychostimulants (though I don't think anyone can say for sure whether or not the psychostimulants caused the brain atrophy the possible link should make prescribers, teachers and parents who are fans of Ritalin stop and think for a moment).

Finally, the company selling Ritalin tells doctors that: 'Data on safety and efficacy of long-term use of Ritalin are not complete.' For this reason they recommend that patients requiring long-term therapy should be monitored carefully with periodic complete and differential blood counts, and platelet counts.

Now, maybe I'm being rather demanding but it does seem to me that when a drug has been on the market since the early 1960s it wouldn't be entirely unreasonable for the drug company involved to have completed studying the data on whether or not it works and is safe.

But, perhaps I'm just being picky.

\* \* \*

As an aside there has been some research done on mice.

When early safety tests were done on mice researchers found that the drug caused an increase in hepatocellular adenomas and, in male mice only, an increase in hepatoblastomas (described as 'a relatively rare rodent malignant tumour type').

'The significance of these results to humans is unknown' say the company selling Ritalin.

Here, once again, is yet more proof of the total worthlessness of animal experiments and the ruthless and cynical attitude shown by drug companies and those government departments which allegedly exist to protect the public from unsafe drugs.

I have frequently argued that when drug companies perform preclinical tests on animals they do so knowing that if the tests show that a drug doesn't cause any problems when given to animals they can use the results to help convince the authorities that the drug is safe.

On the other hand when a drug does cause a problem when given to animals the results can be ignored on the grounds that 'the significance of these results to humans is unknown'.

The question here is a very simple one: if the experiments on mice which showed that Ritalin causes cancer were of value why is the drug still available on prescription for children? And if the experiments can safely be ignored (on the grounds that animals are so different to human beings that the results are irrelevant) why were the tests done in the first place?

I don't expect any answers. I just like asking the questions.

* * *

Whenever I write about Ritalin I am inundated with letters, faxes and e-mails from parents, teachers and social workers insisting that Ritalin is 'very safe'. I suspect these optimistic folk must either be unable to read or too lazy to do any research into the safety of a product which they are recommending with such enthusiasm. Years of experience mean that I am not in the slightest bit surprised to find such crass stupidity exhibited by social workers. I am, however, surprised to find so many school teachers showing such a potent mixture of ignorance and misplaced trust.

Sadly, it seems it is partly through the enthusiasm of teachers and social workers that Ritalin is now so widely prescribed.

In theory Ritalin should not be prescribed for any child unless a doctor has performed a thorough evaluation. However, despite this, when a team of researchers from the United Nationals International Narcotics Control Board examined the records of nearly 400 paediatricians who had prescribed Ritalin they found that half the children who had been diagnosed as suffering from MBD (or ADD or whatever) had not been given psychological or educational testing before being given the drug. The United Nations concluded that frustrated parents, teachers and doctors were too quick to stick a label of ADD onto children with behavioural problems (or, to be more accurate, onto children whose behaviour was annoying the parents, teachers and doctors).

* * *

I am less than enthusiastic about this drug. In my view, the world would be a healthier place if all supplies of the damned stuff were wrapped in concrete and buried. I wouldn't prescribe Ritalin for anyone – for anything.

But other doctors clearly don't agree with me. Some observers have described Ritalin as a drug that can unlock a child's potential. And although estimates about the number of children taking Ritalin vary it has been claimed that in the USA alone up to 12 per cent of all American boys aged between 6 and 14 are being prescribed Ritalin to treat various behavioural disorders. It is now not unknown for schools to arrange for children to be treated with Ritalin without obtaining parental permission.

I've been told that in some cases boys have been given Ritalin because they ran around the playground making a noise. *They ran around the playground making a noise, for heaven's sake!*

It is worth remembering that although doctors, parents and teachers have for over thirty years now been enthusiastically recommending the use of Ritalin (and similar drugs) in the treatment of MBD (or ADHD or XYZ) there are still a number of unanswered questions.

I don't believe anyone definitely knows whether the drug works or whether it causes any permanent long-term damage. I don't believe anyone knows for certain whether the drug does more harm than good. And, perhaps most astonishing of all, despite the fact that millions of children have been diagnosed as suffering from ADHD, ADD or MBD, and treated with powerful drugs, I don't believe we even know whether any of these conditions really exist.

Back in 1970, the Committee on Government Operations of the USA House of Representatives studied the use of behaviour modification drugs on children. At that time around 200,000 to 300,000 children a year in the USA were being given these drugs. The point was made that hyperactivity was considered a disease because it made it difficult for schools to be run 'like maximum security prisons, for the comfort and the convenience of the teachers and administrators who work in them...'.

Since then the only thing that has changed is that the popularity of Ritalin has continued to rise and rise and rise inexorably.

Prescribing Ritalin is, in my view, authorised child abuse on a massive, global scale.

And, sadly, things aren't likely to change.

When, in January 1999, I wrote a paper expressing my doubts about Ritalin (a paper which encouraged several major newspapers to question the wisdom of prescribing this drug so widely) I received an avalanche of angry mail from furious parents, teachers and social workers.

'I'm not going to read your report,' wrote one father of a child on Ritalin. 'I know it's rubbish.'

Most worrying of all is the fact that parents who are reluctant to give their children Ritalin have been told that if they don't give in and cooperate their children will be taken away from them. This will, of course, not be the first example of 'compulsory medication'. In some countries (notably parts of the USA) parents who do not have their children vaccinated are liable to arrest. And, of course, the fluoridation of drinking water is also common in many parts of the world.

## 33 | Water, Water Everywhere – And Not A Drop Fit To Drink

You probably don't think of water as a food but water is just as valuable as anything you eat. A massive 60 per cent to 65 per cent of your body is water. (The figure is even higher for a baby. Approximately 75 per cent of a baby's weight is water). If you didn't eat and didn't drink it would be the shortage of water which killed you first. You could survive for weeks without food but you would be dead within days without water.

However, thanks to doctors the water you get when you turn on your tap probably isn't safe to drink.

Back in 1982, my fears were aroused by one piece of fairly obscure – and widely ignored research – which showed that sewage entering a sewage treatment plant in the USA contained excreted aspirin, caffeine and nicotine and another piece of equally widely ignored research which showed that a cholesterol lowering drug had turned up in a reservoir. The drug had, it seemed, got into the reservoir from treated sewage.

I concluded that every time anyone drank a glass of tap water they were possibly drinking second-hand drugs.

If my theory is right then millions of people now regularly take powerful drugs such as sleeping tablets, painkillers and hormonal contraceptive pills.

The theory is easy to explain.

After a drug has been taken it is metabolized (or broken down) before it is excreted. Some of the most powerful and most widely prescribed drugs leave the body in much the same form as they entered it. For example, 75 per cent of a dose of diazepam (one of the world's most popularly prescribed benzodiazepine tranquillisers) leaves in the urine of the person who has taken it as another version of the drug. A third of a dose of ampicillin (a widely prescribed antibiotic) is excreted in the urine within six hours of the pill or capsule being swallowed.

Once domestic waste water leaves our homes it goes to sewage treatment plants where it is 'purified' using standard techniques (many of them devised and perfected in the nineteenth century) which are intended to remove bacteria and other obvious contaminants. Once these unwanted additions have been removed the apparently 'clean' water goes back into circulation as drinking water. But it isn't clean. It still contains drug residues. And each time the cycle goes round, the concentration of drug residues increases.

Although water purification methods are effective at removing bacteria and obvious waste materials from 'dirty' water the purification processes are not able to remove all the drug and hormone residues from the sewage.

The result is that when allegedly pure domestic waste water is put back into our water supply systems it still contains many different drug residues – chemicals derived from antibiotics, heart drugs, tranquillisers, sleeping pills, antidepressants, painkillers and contraceptive pills. (It also, inevitably, also contains residues of other chemicals – such as toiletries, shampoos, cosmetics and garden and kitchen products).

So, when you turn on your kitchen tap and fill your kettle you could be getting water that contains second-hand tranquillisers, second-hand heart drugs, second-hand contraceptive hormones and other substances. And as the years go so the whole process will get worse and worse. Each time another human being somewhere in the cycle takes another tablet the water you drink becomes more polluted. Much drinking water has already become terribly contaminated with second-hand drugs and I believe that everyone who drinks water which has been purified from sewage effluent or extracted from a river into which sewage effluent has been discharged must be taking small quantities of a large variety of prescription drugs.

Remarkably little research has been done to find out just how significant this problem is but when scientists tested river water they found detectable amounts of progestogen (one of the ingredients of the contraceptive pill) in it. Research carried out in Germany showed that the amount of oestrogen (another ingredient of the contraceptive pill) seems to be increasing in surface water supplies. What effects are all these hormones and drugs having on us? Are we all being tranquillised by second-hand tranquillisers and sleeping tablets? What effect do all these hormone residues have on pregnant women and their developing babies? (After all the manufacturers of many drugs warn that their products should not be given to pregnant women). What effect are all these hormones having on men? Are we creating a new race of intersexual beings?

In the last few years I gradually started to find more research being published on this subject.

American and Canadian scientists published preliminary evidence confirming that traces of drugs, excreted by people and animals on farms, have been found in water in their respective countries.

('At the time,' says one of the new researchers, who obviously missed the paper I wrote for a medical magazine back in 1982, 'we didn't pay attention to the finding. It should have been a wake up call because if one drug could pass through a sewage treatment plant and percolate through soil unscathed, so could a host of other drugs.')

There seems little doubt that drinking water is now heavily contaminated with drug residues. Some of the drugs come from sewage. Some come from unwanted prescription drugs dumped with refuse and leaking into underground water supplies. And some come from farm animal waste. Drinking water supplies in the developed world continue to deteriorate. Drug residues in the water go round and round and round – being added to every time someone else swallows a drug. Since most people are on medication our drinking water is now pretty well undrinkable.

The long-term effect of all this is difficult to estimate. Minute amounts of antibiotic in drinking water can affect bacteria in many different ways. They can surely have a dramatic effect on the development of antibiotic resistant organisms.

There is not yet any firm evidence showing a clear link between water pollution and problems (such as fertility) affecting human beings. But the absence of any such evidence may possibly be a result of the fact that as far as I know no one has yet done any research into this issue. The research would be extremely simple to do and wouldn't cost very much. Given the extent of the circumstantial evidence it is something of a scandal that no one has bothered to do the research that I think is needed.

How are the drugs in your drinking water affecting your health? Is your involuntary daily cocktail of tranquillisers, antibiotics, hormones, steroids, chemotherapy drugs, heart drugs, painkillers and so on making you ill? How do all these drugs interact? Are they likely to be at least partly responsible for the way the incidence of cancer is increasing?

This really is one of the biggest health scandals – and dangers – of the twenty first century. A German researcher has found at least three drugs in water from his tap at home. It is hardly surprising that politicians everywhere are now given bottled water to drink (at our expense, of course).

But why, I wonder, has there been a conspiracy of silence among national newspapers and magazines and TV and radio stations? Back in 1982 producers for several TV and radio programmes cancelled interviews with me (which had been arranged to discuss this problem) because they said it would frighten the public too much. And still no one will cover this problem.

When, right at the end of the twentieth century, a Sunday newspaper carried a news story about the suggestion in my book *Superbody* that drinking water may contain excreted drug residues, spokesmen for the water industry were quick to dismiss my fears. One water company spokesman was reported to have said: 'To suggest water purification programmes are out-dated and not up to the job is quite simply wrong. It's impossible to say there's no drug residues in recycled drinking water but the levels are thousands of times below anything that could cause harm.'

How could that spokesman possibly know how low the levels are when he admits he doesn't know whether there are any drugs in recycled drinking water or not? How does he know that levels are 'thousands of times below anything that could cause harm' when he clearly doesn't know what the levels are? Isn't it about time water companies practised a little science and did some tests to find out exactly what is happening?

Doctors continue to say that there is nothing at all to worry about and that my warnings are unjustified. But it should be remembered that by their overprescribing it is doctors who are a major cause of the problem. It is thanks to your doctor (and his or her colleagues) that the water from your tap may not be fit to drink.

It is also important to remember that the medical profession has firmly allied itself with the financial interests of the international pharmaceutical industry. It is clearly in the interests both of doctors and drug companies for doctors to continue to overprescribe powerful and expensive drugs.

Meanwhile, the circumstantial evidence suggesting the accuracy of my original 1982 warning continues to accumulate and I am now convinced, more than ever, that my warning was (and is) valid.

* * *

The other water pollutant that really should worry us all is, of course, fluoride.

Fluoride is deliberately added to drinking water supplies in the hope that it will help reduce the incidence of tooth decay. The link between fluoride and tooth decay was first established at the end of the nineteenth century and there is little doubt that fluoride does help to protect the teeth by making tooth enamel – the hard outside covering of teeth – tougher and more decay resistant. When tests done on large numbers of people showed that tooth decay is slower in those parts of the country where drinking water supplies naturally contain fluoride some scientists and politicians suggested that putting fluoride into the drinking water supplies might improve the dental health of the general population. The fluoridation of water supplies began in America in 1945, and today the move towards fluoridation is spreading all over the world. Politicians are enthusiastic about using fluoride in this way because they have been convinced that the end result will be a reduction in health costs. (There is nothing politicians love more than to be able to cut the cost of looking after the people while at the same time claiming that what they are doing is for the good of the electorate. It's a double whammy for the modern, crooked politician.)

However, those who oppose fluoridation are able to put forward several arguments in their favour.

First, you do not, of course, have to add fluoride to drinking water in order to protect teeth. You can get exactly the same effect by persuading people to use fluoride toothpastes. And since many toothpastes now do contain fluoride most people already get all the fluoride they need simply by brushing their teeth.

Second, there is no doubt that putting fluoride into drinking water supplies is a potentially dangerous business. The amount of fluoride that you can put into drinking water has to be judged very accurately. To get the best effect from the fluoride you need to add around one part per million. However, if you get the sums wrong the consequences can be devastating. Just two parts of fluoride per million can cause mottling of the teeth and if the quantities are allowed to rise a little higher bone disorders and cancer may be the result. Naturally, the scientists and politicians who are keen on putting fluoride into our drinking water supplies claim that the methods used are foolproof but I think that one would have to be a fool to believe that. Many people have already been poisoned by accidental overdoses of chemicals and in 1986 the World Health Organisation published a report in which concern was expressed about the incidence of dental problems caused by there being *too much* fluoride in public drinking water supplies. Needless to say getting unwanted, excess fluoride out of the drinking water supplies can be extremely difficult. To all this we must add the fact that since drinking water supplies already contain a number of chemicals – some of which occur naturally in the supplies, nitrates which accumulate because of the use of fertilizers, chlorine and aluminium sulphate which are added deliberately and lead or copper from the pipes which are used to supply the water to our homes – adding fluoride to the mixture may increase the risk of a dangerous interaction between the various chemicals in the water. Whenever chemicals exist in solution together there are chemical reactions. I don't think anyone really knows what the consequences are of putting all these chemicals into our drinking water.

The fourth anti-fluoridation argument is that a growing number of people seem to be allergic to the chemicals which are being put into our drinking water. Many people are allergic to fluoride and cannot drink fluoridated drinking water.

Finally, I am particularly worried by the fact that as the pro-fluoridation argument is won in more and more parts of the world, scientists and politicians are suggesting putting other chemicals into the drinking water supplies. One scientist has, for example, already suggested that drinking water should have antibiotics added to it (to reduce the incidence of infection and so to reduce health costs). Another has recommended that tranquillisers be added to drinking water supplies (in order to calm down the voters and allow the politicians to get on with running the world the way they want to run it). A third suggestion has been that contraceptives be added to the drinking water in order to reduce the birth rate.

A surprising number of doctors and politicians support the compulsory fluoridation of water (it is difficult to think of a more fascist act than to force people to take medicine, regardless of their need, whether they want it or not) and in much of the world it seems that this battle is now lost. However, it isn't lost everywhere.

In Switzerland (perhaps the only true democracy remaining in the world) the Swiss Canton of Basel-Stadt recently repealed a resolution on fluoridation which had been introduced in 1962. The Swiss stopped adding fluoride to their water after over 40 years on the following grounds:

1. Although fluoridation has been going on for many decades there are no studies proving that the fluoridation of drinking water prevents tooth decay.

2. Dental caries in the area had increased in children, despite the fluoridation of the drinking water (rather suggesting that the added fluoride hadn't done any good and might be doing harm).

3. The fluoridation of water might cause bone damage – and could be a particular problem in young children and babies.

4. More than 99 per cent of water with added fluoride is used for washing, bathing, cleaning etc. and so does nothing for teeth but does pollute the environment.

\* \* \*

Doctors have now begun to investigate the problem of drug residues in drinking water. Assuming the politicians allow the results to be published (a big assumption) we should know the answers in another decade or so. It will, of course, be far too late to do anything about it by then.

Meanwhile, most people continue to drink far too little water. And many health problems are caused, or made worse, by dehydration.

To avoid this problem try to cut down on alcohol, fizzy drinks and caffeinated teas and coffees. Instead you should drink six to eight decent sized glasses of water a day. If you can't bear the idea of drinking that much water look for drinks that contain no alcohol, no caffeine and no sugar or sodium. Herbal, fruit or mint teas are fine as are decaffeinated drinks. Alternatively you can try drinking pure fruit juice diluted with water. So, meanwhile, while doctors, politicians and the water industry look into a problem they should have been investigating two decades ago, here are some tips on how you can best protect yourself from polluted, drug laden drinking water.

1.  If you suffer from any bizarre or otherwise inexplicable symptoms consider the possibility that your drinking water may be polluted. And it could be the water which is making you ill. This is particularly likely to be the case if you have acquired any new and unusual health problems after recently moving house.

2.  Small babies should be breast fed for as long as possible – ideally for up to twelve months. Breast feeding a baby reduces the risk of the baby being poisoned by polluted water or milk (though it does not reduce the risk to nil since drugs are excreted in breast milk).

3.  If you suspect that any symptoms which you have could be caused by drinking water obtained from a tap try drinking bottled water instead to see if your symptoms disappear. My advice is that you drink bottled water. Remember that bottled drinking water isn't necessarily pure. Some 'spring water' has been purified or chemically treated while the stuff sold as 'table water' may be nothing more than filtered tap water. Try to buy 'natural mineral water' which comes from a protected, pure, unadulterated source and has not been tampered with. Natural mineral water may contain some bacteria (though not usually enough to do you any harm) and so you shouldn't keep bottled natural mineral water lying around once the bottle has been opened. I believe that the chances are good that spring water will remain relatively unpolluted for some years to come. To hedge my bets I drink different brands of bottled water.

4.  If you live in the country and you can do so then you may be better off obtaining your water from a private water supply. But do make sure that you get your water tested before drinking it.

5.  Even if you obtain your water from a commercial company or government owned concern you would be wise to have it tested – as it comes out of the tap.

6.  You can buy table-top filters which remove many contaminants from drinking water. If you buy and use one of these devices make sure that you follow the manufacturers instructions.

7.  If you suspect that your drinking water supplies are of poor quality make your protests heard by your political representatives. Things will never change if you do not protest.

I now suspect that the only real answer is to have two separate metered water supplies – with two inputs to every house. One tap would give out drug contaminated water which could be used for washing up, cleaning cars and flushing lavatories. Water recovered from sewage farms and rivers could be used for this supply. The other tap would give clean, drug free water taken from boreholes, springs and other uncontaminated sources.

## 34 What I Would Do If Doctors Told Me I Had Cancer

I have a one in three chance of being told one day that I have cancer. And you face the same odds. Actually the odds are getting worse. If the incidence of cancer continues to rise at the same rate at which it has risen for the last few years then within a decade or so one in two of us will hear those frightening words – or whichever euphemism our doctor feels most comfortable with.

(To be accurate, because you and I know many of the commonest causes of cancer we have, hopefully, improved our odds considerably. But the risk is still there. However sensibly we live it is impossible to reduce our cancer risk to zero.)

Half a century or so ago approximately one in fourteen could expect to develop cancer. Fifteen years ago that figure had risen to one in four. Governments and charities have spent billions of whatever currency was available to fight cancer and yet none of those responsible for this massive expenditure seem to be in the slightest bit embarrassed by their utter failure. They greet reports of rises in the incidence of cancer with requests for more money – which will, of course, be spent in exactly the same way as all the rest of the money they have been given. More of the same useless research (much of it involving laboratory animals) and more of the same ineffective cancer treatments.

The huge international cancer industry (which raises and spends untold millions of dollars in the constant and in my view futile search for a cure for cancer) has created the impression that cancer is a single disease.

But it isn't. Indeed, it is vitally important to remember that cancer is not a single disease. The word 'cancer' is no more specific than the words 'infection' or 'arthritis'.

And scientists are as unlikely to find a single magic 'cure' for all types of cancer as they are to find a single magic 'cure' for all types of infection. I am annoyed when, just about every week, researchers make great claims for their latest breakthrough. (Little or nothing is ever heard of most of these 'breakthroughs'. I find it difficult to avoid the conclusion that in many cases these widely publicised 'breakthroughs' are little more than fund raising schemes. I find the gullibility of reporters equally annoying. This constant promise of a 'cure around the corner' simply helps to ensure that most people remain passive about cancer; happy to do nothing either to protect themselves or to help treat themselves because they believe that scientists will soon have a magic remedy in a bottle with which it will be possible to conquer cancer.)

If I was told that I had cancer I would not be willing to put my future in the hands of the promises made by some anonymous and grant hungry white coated scientists.

I would want to take some control over my own destiny by following a combination programme that would combine the healing powers of my body and my mind.

And because I would undoubtedly be shocked and frightened (and possibly not too capable of rational thought) it seems to me sensible to make some plans now. It is a lot easier to be rational and logical about an emotional issue like cancer when you are feeling fit and healthy. It seems to me to make more sense to prepare for this eventuality now – rather than at a time when I might be frightened and shocked to know what to do. I have planned for my old age (in case I am too frail and weak to work and earn a living). It seems to me to make equal good sense to plan for the possibility that I may one day develop cancer. I may never need to use my cancer plan – just as I may never need to use my retirement plan. But it is good to know that they are there.

I have tried to create a truly holistic anti-cancer plan; taking the best from many different forms of medicine. This plan is built upon my philosophy of medicine and of life and of living.

It is important to understand that I do not suggest that my programme will or could be suitable for everyone. I do not even recommend it to you. What you decide to do if you are ever told that you have cancer has to be your choice. You may decide that you dislike my entire programme. You may prefer to put your faith in doctors who offer surgery, chemotherapy or radiotherapy, or some mixture of the three. You may think that my anti-cancer programme makes good sense and is something that you yourself would like to follow.

* * *

The medical profession's approach to the treatment of cancer is supposed to be logical and scientific. The lack of warmth displayed by surgeons and physicians is frequently excused with the argument that doctors have to remain cold, aloof and distant from their patients in order to provide analytical and dispassionate advice. If doctors came into emotional contact with their patients, so the argument goes, they would lose their objective approach and be unable to act as scientists. This, I am afraid, is nonsense for despite the claims that doctors make, the truth is that orthodox medicine is not a science.

I can support this seemingly controversial observation with several distinct arguments.

First, if orthodox doctors were really scientists they would only use treatments which they had good reason to expect would prove to be advantageous. And before using a treatment they would want to look at research work showing that the treatment was effective and likely to do more good than harm.

This simply isn't the case.

Many patients are surprised to discover just how inadequately medical treatments are tested.

The simple truth is that most doctor-patient encounters are experiments and when doctors prescribe or operate on their patients they usually do so more in the hope than in the expectation that the patient will benefit from the experience.

If you feel sceptical about this assertion then let me remind you that an editorial in the *British Medical Journal* (one of the most respected 'establishment' medical journals in the world) has reported that 'only about 15 per cent of medical interventions are supported by solid scientific evidence'. Looked at the other way this means, of course, that a staggering 85 per cent of medical interventions are not supported by solid scientific evidence. The same editorial also 'confessed' that 'only 1 per cent of the articles in medical journals are scientifically sound'. (In other words, 99 per cent of the articles in medical journals are *not* scientifically sound.)

Next, if doctors used a truly scientific method when treating their patients they would happily use whichever form of treatment seemed to offer their patients the best chance of recovery. And they would use scientific methods to compare the effectiveness of orthodox methods (such as surgery, drugs and radiotherapy) with the effectiveness of unorthodox methods (such as diet).

Doctors do not do this.

When patients recover from cancer while or after receiving orthodox medical therapy (usually one or more of the triumvirate of surgery, drugs or radiotherapy) doctors invariably claim that those patients have got better because of the therapy they have received. And, of course, any patient who survives for five years is said to have been cured. Doctors are always quick to claim the credit when they can.

However, doctors are far more sceptical when patients recover from 'alternative' or 'non-orthodox' remedies. When patients recover from cancer while or after receiving unorthodox therapy (such as a particular type of diet) they are usually said to have recovered 'in spite' of the treatment they have received. Patients who get better after unorthodox therapy are said to have been misdiagnosed or to have made an 'unexplained and spontaneous recovery'. (No patient in history has ever made an 'unexplained and spontaneous recovery' while or after receiving orthodox therapy). Patients who survive for five years after alternative therapy are said to be merely in remission, awaiting a relapse.

And although orthodox doctors are invariably derisive when alternative therapists write about individual patients or describe isolated case histories this is exactly what orthodox doctors themselves do. It is not at all uncommon for medical journals to contain articles and letters based upon experiences with one or maybe two patients.

The medical establishment always tends to oppose anything new and original which threatens the status quo. When the disorder in question is as serious and as badly treated as cancer, this arrogance and reluctance to even consider something new becomes rather close to deceit and professional recklessness. I could put forward a strong case to charge the medical establishment with manslaughter for its continued refusal even to acknowledge or investigate alternative methods of tackling cancer (methods which do not involve drugs, surgery or radiotherapy). The treatment methods offered by doctors are often the only methods patients know about simply because other, less conventional approaches have either been totally suppressed or sneered at and derided so successfully that no one gives them any credence.

Most convincing of all, however, is the fact that practising physicians and surgeons invariably base their own treatment programmes upon their own (usually completely unscientific) views of what will be best for their patients. Despite the availability of clear evidence showing the efficacy of diet, stress control and modest exercise in the treatment (as well as the prevention) of cardiac disease most doctors still insist on treating all their heart patients with either surgery or drug therapy. And despite the existence of other, far more logical options, most doctors still insist that the only way to treat cancer is to attack it from the outside – rather than to help the body heal and protect itself.

If orthodox medicine was truly scientific then patients with the same symptoms would all receive the same treatment. They don't. There are almost as many different treatment programmes on offer as there are doctors in practice. If a patient who has been diagnosed as having a particular type of cancer visits three doctors then it's a pretty safe bet that he or she will be offered three quite different types of advice. Many 'official' anti-cancer programmes, accepted by the medical establishment, can reasonably be described as irrational and illogical. The survival of individual patients sometimes seems to be more a matter of luck than a matter of science. Doctors simply don't understand why when two patients are given a treatment one will die and one will live. It never occurs to them that there may be some other factor involved and that the death of one patient and the survival of the other may be quite unrelated to the medical treatment which was given.

The logical, scientific approach to any problem is always to tackle the cause rather than the symptoms. If your car has a leaky radiator hose it makes far more logical sense to replace the leaky hose than to keep on filling up the radiator with water. If your house roof is leaking it is far more logical to repair the leak than to put out a bucket to catch the drips.

Good doctors do sometimes follow this logical approach.

When the bad doctor sees a patient with indigestion he will simply prescribe an antacid remedy – knowing that it will temporarily relieve the patient's symptoms – and send the patient away.

When a good doctor sees a patient with indigestion he will want to find out what is causing the indigestion. He will investigate the patient's diet and other lifestyle habits in a search for a cause. And he will want to deal with the cause of the symptoms, rather than the symptoms themselves.

Sadly, most doctors still treat cancer in a strangely illogical and senseless way.

Apart from telling cancer patients who smoke to give up their cigarettes, and advising patients with skin cancer to keep out of the sun, most doctors seem far more concerned with attacking the symptoms than with dealing with the cause of their cancer.

The average doctor treating a cancer patient will simply want to attack the cancer with a knife, a drug or radiotherapy. This is like refilling the car radiator when the radiator hose is leaking, or putting a bucket under a leaky roof: it doesn't address the primary cause of the problem.

And yet this is absurd. Cancer is not a specific disease. Removing the lumps and tumours of a cancer does nothing towards attacking the source and cause of the cancer. One of the reasons why cancer develops is that the body's immune system has broken down. In order to tackle cancer effectively the immune system must be encouraged to fight the cancer. The body must be given a chance to tackle the problem which has, after all, been created by its own cells.

When a cancer recurs it isn't necessarily because the surgeon, the radiotherapist or the physician prescribing the chemotherapy has failed to kill all the cancer cells (this is the excuse usually given by surgeons, radiotherapists and physicians and since I try to retain an open mind I will happily agree that it may sometimes be true) but because nothing in the body has changed. The circumstances which led to the development of a first cancer can just as easily lead to the development of a second cancer. The body is simply vulnerable to cancer.

It is for this reason that one often hears of extremely unfortunate individuals who have developed two or even three cancers in separate organs.

When this happens it is, I believe, because the cause of the cancer is within the patient.

It is because the cancer industry either fails to understand this (or doesn't want to believe it) that the cancer industry will never succeed in beating cancer.

All those billions of dollars being pumped into cancer research are being wasted because scientists and doctors insist on attacking an enemy they cannot see.

It is no coincidence that doctors and researchers involved in the cancer industry frequently describe themselves as being involved in a war – that is exactly how they plan their treatment programmes.

But the real problem for the cancer industry is that the real enemy isn't just invisible – it simply doesn't exist in the same way that smallpox, tuberculosis or influenza exist. The real problem, the real enemy which has to be confronted, is not a bunch of malignant cells but a weakened, toxin infiltrated body. And since cancer develops when a body is ill and weak it seems pretty obvious to me that the very last thing the body needs when it is ill is to be attacked with toxic chemicals. Prescribing toxic chemotherapy is like prescribing a hammer blow to the head for a man with a headache. The main hope is that the blow to the head will cause so much pain that he won't notice the original headache.

(The real irony here, as I have mentioned before, is the fact that the same huge multinational corporations which produce the toxic chemicals which cause cancer also sell the toxic chemicals which are prescribed as a 'cure'. This is the ultimate self-serving perpetual motion money machine; exclusively self-serving.)

Orthodox cancer treatment is neither logical nor scientific and it is important to understand and accept this.

(Curiously many doctors respond to criticism of their profession's approach to cancer as though it was a personal affront, claiming that those who dare to reveal their scepticism in public are depriving patients of hope and are insulting hard working medical professionals. It is rare for doctors to acknowledge that the profession's grotesque failure to combat the ever rising tide of cancer patients could be due to the fact that the medical profession has hunted for cures in the wrong places.)

* * *

Most doctors are terrible at telling people bad news because they themselves don't know how to cope with illness. And they certainly don't know how to cope with death. They shut themselves off from any emotional contact with their patients because they don't have the faintest idea about how to face death.

We all feel slightly uncomfortable about the fact that we will die one day. We don't very much like to talk about the prospect of our own death or, indeed, even to think about it. We tend to avoid the subject or to make jokes to try and hide our true feelings. And we don't very much like discussing other people's mortality either. You probably felt slightly queasy and uncomfortable when you read the headline at the top of this chapter. (Perhaps you would have felt even more uncomfortable if the headline had read: 'What You Should Do If You Are Told You Have Cancer').

The problem is that the average doctor isn't any different to you. Doctors feel the same mixture of emotions as you do when you think about death (fear, guilt, regret, anger and so on). And so doctors frequently say really crass things when they're trying to deal with patients who have cancer. (See, for example, Chapter 1.)

If you are prepared for your doctor to be gauche and inept when he or she tells you that you have cancer then you will be much better able to cope with the situation. If you don't expect too much then you won't be hurt or frightened by the absence of any real warmth or human contact.

If I was visiting a doctor and expecting to receive results of tests or investigations which may provide serious news of any kind (not just cancer) I would take someone with me. And that someone would, ideally, be strong and capable. I would want someone with me who could ask questions and remember what the doctor has said but who could also hold my hand when, and for as long as, I needed it held.

I would not try to comfort myself with the thought that doctors are going to be more capable, more scientific or more sensitive in a year or two's time.

(And I would not kid myself that *my* doctor – however long I have known him/her – is going to be any better than the rest of the profession. Most people think that their doctor is special. ('I'm seeing the best surgeon in the country'. 'My doctor looks after all the top people in the area. He's very highly respected.') This is natural. No one wants to think that their doctor is an incompetent fool. And yet the inescapable truth is that doctors have treated cancer badly for decades. They aren't going to improve this year or next year. It is probably safest to assume that they aren't ever going to improve.)

Making a diagnosis and monitoring the way an illness is going are the things orthodox doctors are really good at. Some alternative therapists do claim to be able to make diagnoses (for example through Kirlian photography or iridology) but I can see no point at all in using these techniques. Blood tests, X-rays and CAT scans aren't always right but they are *usually* right. Even if I was committed to using alternative techniques for the treatment of a cancer I would use orthodox techniques to diagnose it accurately and to keep track of what was happening to it.

\* \* \*

The doctor who tells me I have cancer may be an expert. He may be widely respected. He may have treated thousands of patients. He may wear an expensive suit, drive a Mercedes and have an extensive private practice. But there is a very good chance that he will be completely out of date.

Most doctors treat their patients according to their own whims and prejudices. There are still doctors around who routinely cut off the breasts of women with breast cancer. When you ask them why they perform such savage surgery when all the existing evidence shows, quite clearly, that in most cases a lumpectomy produces a better result they will become very defensive and claim that their experience shows otherwise. If you have the courage and strength to push them further on this they will eventually admit that they have never sat down and assessed their results in a scientific way. They do what they do because it is what they've done for years.

So I would go to my local public library and ask someone there to do a computer search for all the latest scientific papers dealing with my disease. I would then order copies of all the relevant journals. Now I admit that I have an advantage over you here because I know some of the language doctors use. But it is a much smaller advantage than you might imagine. One of the best review articles I've ever read about prostate cancer was written by a successful company boss who didn't have any medical training but did his own research. Remember, you don't have to learn about lots of diseases; you only have to learn about one disease.

Many of the journal articles would probably turn out to be disappointing and useless. But one or two might provide nuggets of useful information. And when I'd read a few journal papers I would probably know as much or more about my disease than the doctor who was supposed to be treating me knows about it. If my research produced the names of drugs being used for the treatment of my particular type of cancer I would then ask the library to see if they could dig out any medical reference books containing information about those prescription drugs. I would, in particular, be looking for details of side effects. If the library couldn't get me the information I wanted I would ask my doctor to obtain the information I needed from the drug company making the product. (The drug company will probably only give this information to prescribing doctors). I would repeat the library search for new material every few months in order to make sure that I did not miss any development that might be important to me.

* * *

I don't know about you but if I'm buying a new motor car I do some research before I buy. I check out the various possibilities. I compare and contrast. I look for problems. I look for weaknesses. I don't accept the recommendation of the first salesman I see.

Dealing with cancer is obviously considerably more important than choosing a new car.

And so once I had done some preliminary research into my disease I would ask my GP to arrange two more consultations with experts. Many doctors don't like patients obtaining views from more than one doctor. (This is because they know that other doctors are likely to offer different views about the best possible treatment – thereby making it clear that they just might be wrong.) But I wouldn't worry about my doctor being hurt or offended. That is his problem and I'd have too much to do to worry about his feelings of inadequacy.

I am aware that obtaining these opinions would probably cost me money. (For reasons which you can easily understand state health services and health insurance companies don't always look upon the idea of second and third opinions with much enthusiasm. I am therefore, already making sure that I keep a small nest egg put on one side so that, if necessary, I will have the cash I need to do my research.)

Having done my preliminary research I would be able to ask the expert sensible and searching questions. At the end of the consultation I would ask him this question: 'What would you do if you had what I've got?'

\* \* \*

Doctors treating cancer patients usually offer one of more of these three options: surgery, radiotherapy or drugs (the dreaded trio more commonly known as 'slash, burn and poison').

Good doctors will readily admit that there are often unpleasant side effects with these types of treatment. Surgery is invariably painful and often disfiguring. Patients are frequently mutilated for no very good reason.

Chemotherapy, which is surely one of the crudest and bluntest of all medical techniques, often results in devastating symptoms such as nausea and sickness as well as relatively trivial but potentially dispiriting (and therefore spiritually damaging) symptoms such as hair loss. Battering the entire body with drugs in this clumsy and imprecise way will surely one day be regarded as a major low point of twenty first century medicine (which, admittedly, has many other low points).

Chemotherapy works by poisoning cancer cells. If the drugs only poisoned the cancer cells this would be wonderful. But the problem is that normal cells also die. Chemotherapy drugs are so toxic that they kill just about everything they reach. The prescribing doctor has to carefully adjust the dose of the drug he is prescribing so as to kill the cancer cells without killing too many of the body's essential cells. This is by no means an exact science. Indeed, it isn't really a science at all. It's guesswork and hope. The concept of chemotherapy pays no attention at all to the body's in-built defence mechanisms. On the contrary chemotherapy reduces the effectiveness of the body's defence system and therefore makes it easier for a cancer to grow. Virtually all chemotherapy drugs are immunosuppressive (thereby destroying the body's self-defence mechanisms) and carcinogenic (subsequently producing additional, new cancers). Possible side effects known to be associated with chemotherapy may include: nausea, vomiting, bleeding, loss of hair, liver damage, kidney damage, increased risk of infection, impotence, sterility, bone marrow damage, nerve damage, lung damage, diarrhoea, skin sores, mouth sores, heart damage, allergies and fever. And, of course, an increased susceptibility to another type of cancer.

Drugs mask problems rather than deal with them directly. They do not deal with the disease process. They are unnatural. They contaminate the patient and produce an array of confusing side effects. They cover up symptoms which might be of use in leading the doctor to a better form of treatment.

As for radiotherapy – well, I suspect that it kills more people than it saves.

I had a letter this week from a British patient who had a cancerous growth. 'The cancer was removed by a surgeon who told me that the cancer had not spread,' she wrote. 'But doctors want me to have radiotherapy. Why?'

The answer is simple and shocking.

Radiotherapists want to prove that radiotherapy works and there is at present surprisingly little evidence for its effectiveness.

The current way to measure the effectiveness of treatments is to see how many patients survive for five years after diagnosis.

By giving treatment to patients who may not really need it – and who are likely to make a full recovery whether or not they receive treatment – doctors can make their pet therapy look good.

But radiotherapy can be extremely dangerous.

Amazingly there are no firm rules about who must get radiotherapy – or how much they should receive.

This is a scandal of monumental proportions.

So, how do doctors decide who gets radiotherapy and how much they get?'

If you don't want to know look away now.

Because the answer may frighten you.

They guess.

Radiotherapy is a lottery and (like chemotherapy) about as logical as standing in the garden chanting to the moon.

Don't ever let any doctor tell you that alternative medicine is unscientific.

* * *

What has happened?

Why has a powerful legacy of scientific thought been allowed to crumble away?

Why has twenty first century medicine drifted back towards witchcraft and black arts?

The answer is simple.

In the last century the practice of medicine has become no more than an adjunct to the pharmaceutical industry. Medicine is no longer an independent profession.

Doctors are no more dedicated to the saving of lives and the improvement of patients' welfare than are the thousands of drug company salesmen and marketing men. Doctors have become nothing more than a link connecting the pharmaceutical industry to the consumer.

The end result of this modern tragedy is that patients suffer.

The overprescribing, the unnecessary surgery and the exhausting and endless tests and investigations all weaken patients, damage their immune systems and increase their chances of falling ill.

But few doctors will point out that orthodox treatments for cancer may actually reduce a patient's chance of surviving.

Surgery can (particularly if performed clumsily) result in the spreading of a cancer, and taking a biopsy of a suspected cancer can make things considerably worse. On top of these specific and practical risks there is the fact that the human body is a delicate and vulnerable organism. Chopping bits out is traumatic to the physical form as well as to the psyche. Surgery is an 'insult' to the body. A lengthy operation can weaken the body and reduce its ability to fight cancer. The last thing a body fighting a cancer needs is a surgical operation. And so the reasons for the surgery would have to be convincing. And radiotherapy and chemotherapy may result in a patient's death not just as a result of a serious side effect but also as a result of the damage done to the whole organism's ability to fight and survive.

Nevertheless, I would not dismiss the options of surgery, radiotherapy and chemotherapy completely. If I had a discrete, isolated, accessible and easily removable tumour which was threatening my life through its existence I would consider finding a good surgeon to remove it. I would consider specific radiotherapy aimed directly at a cancer site. I would be extremely cautious about chemotherapy and would consider this option only if I saw extremely convincing evidence proving its efficacy in the treatment of my type of cancer.

The essence of holistic therapy is to retain an open mind about all types of treatment – including so-called orthodox therapy.

* * *

At the same time as I was doing research to find out what orthodox medicine knew about my disease I would also ask my local librarian to do a computer search for alternative remedies.

There are a number of excellent alternative journals now available around the world.

I would want to see as many as possible of these journals. And I would want to look at all the relevant claims made by therapists. (In other words I would want to look at claims which related to my specific type of cancer).

I would, however, be just as sceptical about alternative therapies as I would be about orthodox therapies.

Sadly, the world of alternative medicine is not totally populated by honest, kind and well-meaning individuals. There are some charlatans around whose sole interest is making money. And although I have absolutely no objection to healers and therapists making money if they are offering a good service I would not want to waste money and time on treatments which had little or no chance of working.

(Some orthodox doctors dismiss all alternative therapists as being 'only in it for the money' because they charge a fee. This is, of course, a nonsense. All the orthodox doctors I know get paid. If they don't get paid by individual patients they get paid by the state or by insurance companies. If a therapist offers me a genuine cure for my cancer I will happily pay him whatever I can afford.)

One alternative anti-cancer programme which I would look at very carefully is the one devised by Dr Gerson. The Gerson programme includes the regular consumption of fresh drinks made from vegetables and fruit – and the avoidance of meat, fish, eggs, dairy produce, caffeine, alcohol, salt, nicotine, fats, processed foods, chocolate, spices and ordinary drinking water out of the tap. (I understand, however, that the traditional Gerson programme does, however, include the consumption of liver from very young calves. I do not understand the need for this and would not follow this part of the programme.) I am totally convinced that the regular consumption of fresh fruit and vegetables would make an important difference if I had cancer but I am less convinced about the importance of the castor oil and the coffee enemas (taken to help detoxify the body). One important study of Gerson patients, which was published in the American journal *Alternative Therapies in Health Medicine* in September

1995, showed that 100 per cent of patients with early melanomas survived for five years. A much less substantial 79 per cent of patients who were treated with conventional medicine survived for five years. Of the patients who had regional metastases 70 per cent of the Gerson patients recovered whereas only 41 per cent of the patients given orthodox treatment survived. But it was the severely ill patients who showed the most dramatic results for whereas 39 per cent of Gerson treated patients with distant metastases lived five years (the period which officially defines a 'cure') only six per cent of the patients who were treated with orthodox medical therapies survived for that long. And yet, tragically, despite this evidence, the cancer establishment (composed of both doctors who are supposed to be driven by a desire to find the best therapies for their patients and cancer charities which are given money to find 'cures' for cancer) still refuses to accept the Gerson programme – or even to subject it to more tests.

\* \* \*

One woman, investigating an anti-cancer programme that would have entailed considerable effort on her part rejected the programme on the grounds that it would interfere with her lifestyle.

But since it was probably her original lifestyle which had resulted in the development of the cancer would a change in lifestyle have been such a bad thing?

The important question, of course, is just how big a price are you prepared to pay to defeat the cancer?

There are times in our lives when we have to face reality and we have to take responsibility for our own actions. And facing cancer is such a time. This is not a time to put your fate into the hands of a doctor whose only virtue is that his ignorance is heavily disguised by arrogance and conceit. Making the decision about what to do – and how to tackle the disease – is a difficult one.

If I choose not to accept orthodox medicine and I die – did I make a mistake? If I choose to accept orthodox medicine and I die after several months of pain and misery did I make a mistake? Life is all about choices and decisions and this, I believe, is a choice we have to make for ourselves.

\* \* \*

It is a constant disappointment to me that the majority of doctors (and, indeed, patients) will not accept that there is a link between food and cancer.

I don't remember being taught anything at all about the links between food and cancer when I was a medical student so I suppose it isn't all that surprising that the majority of doctors in practise today think that anyone claiming that such a relationship exists must be a crank and possibly a charlatan too.

(The extent of the opposition to the simple and well proven link between food and cancer is well illustrated by what happened in the UK when my book *Food for Thought* first came out just a few years ago. To launch the book to the public the EMJ advertising department bought advertisement space in a number of British newspapers. The advertisement used made it clear that the book contained information about foods which are linked to cancer (either because they cause cancer or because they help to prevent it. Shortly after the advertisement had appeared we received notification from a British organisation known as the Advertising Standards Authority that there had been a complaint about the advertisement.

Our advertisement had included the statement: 'In his bestselling book *Food for Thought* Dr Vernon explains which foods to avoid and which to eat to reduce your risk of developing cancer.' The ASA asked us to provide evidence for this claim and we were happy to help relieve their ignorance. We sent a short list of basic references. We pointed out that the National Academy of Sciences in the United States estimates that 60 per cent of women's cancers and 40 per cent of men's cancers are related to nutritional factors. We also gave details of and included references for papers which had been published in the following specialist cancer journals: *Cancer*, *Cancer Research*, *International Journal of Cancer*, *British Journal of Cancer* and the *New England Journal of Medicine*.

We also pointed out that the British Medical Association had published a book stating that one third of cancers are caused by food. And we suggested that the ASA might like to look at *Nutritional Influences on Illness* by Dr Melvyn R Werbach – an excellent reference source book which contains 18 pages of references showing links between specific foods and cancer. We sent references and details of these publications because we were informed that photocopying all these publications would have been illegal. But the ASA said that they would not accept scientific references. And, working I believe, with the help of medical advice, they duly banned the advertisement which dared to suggest that there are links between food and cancer.)

Although there is plenty of evidence showing that there are links between food and cancer (showing that while some foods cause cancer others can help prevent it) there is not yet any equally convincing scientific evidence proving that eating the right sort of foods can cure cancer.

And yet it is perfectly logical that it should be possible to combat cancer by eating the right sort of foods. After all, if avoiding some types of food can help you avoid cancer it doesn't take much brainpower to conclude that it makes good sense to avoid those foods if you have developed cancer.

Hard, scientific evidence supporting the belief that cancer can be defeated by eating the right sort of diet hasn't yet been produced for the simple (but awful) reason that it is in no one's interest to produce any such evidence.

The cancer industry (which raises billions of dollars in public contributions) is run by doctors who are committed to an orthodox 'slash, burn and poison' approach to cancer – the approach they have been educated to accept. They will not make any effort to assess the effectiveness of diet in treating cancer because there is no evidence that such an approach would work. It is a vicious circle of denial. 'There is no evidence that diet cures cancer and therefore we cannot justify doing the extensive and costly research that could prove that diet cures cancer and so there is no evidence that diet cures cancer.'

Why are doctors so opposed even to considering the idea that cancer may be tackled (and prevented) by diet? The subject is hardly ever even mentioned by doctors and only rare is it discussed at medical meetings or in journals. The food served in hospitals is consistently reported to be appalling. There are many hospitals where meat is still regarded as an essential part of a main meal and where fruit (if served at all) is served from tins, and vegetables are overcooked into a soggy, unidentifiable mass. Those doctors who do dare to offer the suggestion that the right sort of diet is an important pre-requisite for good health are largely regarded as cranks, to be reviled and ignored.

I suspect that the real reason for the opposition to the notion of maintaining or regaining good health through sensible eating is that the medical profession is largely controlled and educated by the pharmaceutical industry – which has a clear financial interest in maintaining the theory that cancer is best tackled with the aid of chemotherapy. And we must also remember that the treatment of cancer patients is big business. Around $20,000,000,000 a year are spent on conventional cancer treatments in the United States of America alone. I'm not suggesting that all those involved in the cancer industry are consciously refusing even to test new ideas simply because they are worried about being made redundant. But that unspoken fear is undoubtedly there and it doubtless influences some. Changing the way we approach cancer would result in mass unemployment in hospitals, drug companies, laboratories, cancer charities and other parts of the huge cancer industry.

Never before in the history of man has the medical establishment demanded (and received) so much money to tackle cancer. Cancer charities are now the biggest and richest charities in the world. Presidents and Prime Ministers around the world have proudly announced that *their* administration will conquer cancer.

And yet, despite all this effort, the incidence of cancer continues to rise. A few years ago one in three people got cancer. Today the figure is close to one in two. The medical establishment's approach to cancer has failed miserably. The cancer charities have failed miserably. And, despite their boastful rhetoric, governments have failed miserably.

Why?

The broad answer is simple and comes in three parts.

First: these establishment forces have all been busy working with drug companies and have all insisted on tackling the problem of cancer by searching for a single, pharmacological cure. Billions of dollars have been spent on the search for a magic bullet cure for cancer: a drug or a vaccine that will cure or prevent cancer the easy way. Governments, charities and doctors have spent most of their energy (and a good deal of public money) on helping drug companies look for a hugely profitable solution to this problem.

Second: the same establishment forces have steadfastly refused to face the fact that the vast majority of cancers are caused by chemicals in the food we eat, the air we breathe and the water we drink. The big chemical companies have contaminated our world with known carcinogens. The politicians daren't say anything because these are big, rich companies. And the medical establishment and the charities daren't say anything because their pockets are stuffed with money from drug companies which are often affiliated to, associated with, or subsidiaries of, the big companies making and selling the carcinogens. The result is that millions of innocent people are allowed and encouraged to expose themselves to cancer risks which could often be easily avoided.

Third: while the battle against cancer is inspired, driven by and controlled by a fruitless search for a hugely profitable cancer cure the establishment has failed to put much effort at all into explaining to people the importance and significance of the human immune system. Millions would avoid cancer if their immune systems were in better condition. And millions would recover from cancer if they were told how to boost their immune systems.

Indeed, I believe that the cancer industry hasn't just failed to explain the importance of the immune system – it has done its aggressive best to discourage cancer patients (and potential cancer victims) from discovering the truth about the significance of the immune system.

At grass roots level millions of patients have been betrayed because their doctors have failed to realise that their own education has been dominated by a drug industry dominated establishment which cares far more for profits than it does for patient care.

Visit your doctor as a cancer patient and the chances are that you'll be offered one or more choices from the unholy trilogy: chemotherapy, surgery and radiotherapy. And yet the track record for these 'weapons' against cancer is truly abysmal. It is, indeed, so bad that I suspect that if many varieties of chemotherapy were offered by an alternative practitioner as a 'cure for cancer' he would be arrested for fraud.

The bottom line is that I believe that the best way to avoid cancer (and the best way to defeat it if you get it) is to do everything you can to boost your immune system. I've explained my programme for doing this in some detail in my book *Superbody*.

(Of course, strengthening the immune system isn't the only way to attack cancer and the truly holistic approach which I favour accepts that everything (even chemotherapy, radiotherapy and surgery) may on occasion be useful and effective.)

Having studied the evidence I can find, I have absolutely no doubt that by eating a diet which contains a great deal of fresh, organically grown fruit and fresh and organically grown vegetables (a diet which is, therefore, rich in antioxidants) but which contained very little fat I would be giving my body every chance to defeat its enemy. And I would keep my calorie intake fairly low. Since there are clear links between overweight and cancer I would certainly not want to put on any excess weight through overeating.

I would want to make sure that I eschewed all chemicals (whether used in the farming process or added by food manufacturers) since I am totally convinced that it is the high incidence of chemicals in our diet and in our environment which is mainly responsible for the increase in cancer in the world today.

I already follow a vegetarian diet and so I eat no animal produce. But if I was not a vegetarian I would become one. The evidence linking meat and fats to the development of cancer is irresistible (I summarised many of the most important scientific papers showing a link between diet and cancer in my book *Food for Thought*).

I believe there is a strong link between animal fat and cancer because it is in the fat of an animal that the chemicals it has consumed are likely to be found. People who eat a fat rich diet are, therefore, consuming a greater quantity of cancer provoking toxins. Not surprisingly, the last thing someone with cancer needs is to consume a diet which contains more cancer provoking toxins. Anyone who eats the wrong diet will suffer twice: their body will be weakened and handicapped while their cancer is aided and abetted.

One writer recently claimed that obtaining enough vitamins and minerals from fruit and vegetables would require eating impossibly large quantities of food. It was also alleged that it is impossible to find organic food in most cities. I think that both these claims are quite wrong. A diet which contains five different servings of fruit and vegetables (with variation from day to day of course) should provide a thoroughly extensive variety of vitamins and minerals. And I don't know of a city where it isn't possible to buy organic food. The quickest way to find a shop or farm selling organic food is usually to visit a vegetarian restaurant and ask for their help.

Finding organically grown fruit and vegetables may require a little effort (and the produce may cost slightly more) but the effort is well worthwhile.

Others have complained that fresh fruit and vegetables are expensive to buy. I suppose they probably are more expensive than many pre-packaged foods. But if you eat in a healthy fashion you will not spend money on meat, fatty foods such as cream, sweets and the other mass produced foods with which so many people conscientiously and steadfastly ruin their health.

I prefer to obtain vitamins and antioxidants through food. I think that this is the healthy and sensible way to feed the body. But I would also take vitamin supplements adding to my daily intake of antioxidants.

The important thing to remember is that cancer results from a general metabolic disturbance. And, therefore, I believe that in order to effect a cure it is essential to provide a general remedy.

Most people in the developed world eat too much food but are malnourished. The food they eat is fatty, full of additives and chemicals and poor in vitamins and minerals. Even the water which comes out of our taps, and which we are expected to drink, is often heavily polluted with chemicals.

But it isn't only poor food that causes cancer. Another factor is, I believe, our constant exposure to a polluted environment. The very air we breathe is frequently heavily polluted. Our bodies, weakened by poor food and too much stress, simply cannot cope with the enormous quantities of pollutants and contaminants. If I developed cancer I would make every effort to ensure that I breathed clean air and kept away (as far as possible) from cancer-provoking environmental toxins. And so, for example, if I lived in a town or city I would try to spend as much time as possible in the countryside.

\* \* \*

There are powerful links between stress, the human body's immune system and the development of cancer. When the mind is under a great deal of stress the body becomes weaker and more vulnerable and less able to protect itself against cancer.

And so it doesn't take a great deal of intellect to realise that when a cancer has developed, and the body is fighting hard to stop those errant cells multiplying and causing havoc, the strength and health of the immune system is absolutely vital.

Eating the right sort of foods is, of course, one vital ingredient in the recipe for a healthy immune system. But avoiding unnecessary stress is also vital. The therapeutic value of peace and dignity are grossly undervalued by many health care professionals.

(It is for this reason that the stress produced by surgery may be counterproductive. The benefit of removing a tumour has to be carefully weighed against the damage that may be done to the immune system. Most surgeons do not do this because they do not even know that these links between stress, immune system and cancer exist.)

There is even evidence to show that simply worrying about external forces may prove damaging to the immune system.

There is, for example, evidence showing that people who live near to nuclear power stations may have an increased incidence of cancer not solely because of the radiation which is emitted from the power station but also because of the stress created by living near to a possible source of radiation.

It seems pretty certain that the people who worry most about themselves, their families, their friends, their work and the rest of the world in general are the ones who suffer most.

There is no little irony in the fact that hard-hearted folk who ignore the effects of what they do to other people, animals or the environment because they simply do not care two hoots about the consequences do not suffer much in the way of damaging stress. It is the kind, the thoughtful and the sensitive who suffer for them − and whose immune systems take a battering as a result of their actions.

In addition to minimising my exposure to stress I would also spend more time making sure that I could relax my body and my mind quite thoroughly. I would also make the effort to meditate regularly − using the sort of techniques described in my book *Mindpower*.

I firmly believe that having a positive, relaxed and contented mind greatly improves the capacity of the body to recover from any illness.

\* \* \*

Simply wanting to stay alive is not a big enough reason not to die. I know that in order to combat cancer I would need to have a real purpose for living.

When I was a GP I saw many patients who defied medical forecasts simply because they could not and would not die. Two women (whose case histories I described in more detail in my book *Mindpower*) both quite simply refused to die because they had children who needed looking after. They clung to life with dogged determination because for them death was not an acceptable option.

One of the first things I would do would be to sit down and make a written list of my short, medium and long-term purposes, aims and ambitions.

I know that it would not be enough to simply write down vague and uncertain hopes and aspirations. I would define my aims quite specifically – listing the projects I wanted to complete and giving each project a timescale.

I would keep my short-term projects to a minimum (because I know that I would be spending much of my time, effort and energy fighting the cancer). I would, however, make an extensive list of medium and long-term ambitions. Those projects and ambitions would give my life a renewed purpose.

* * *

I first described the power of visualisation therapy in my books *Bodypower* (first published in 1983) and *Mindpower* (first published in 1987). Astonishingly, this enormously important form of self-treatment is still largely unknown among doctors.

Since the effective practice of visualisation therapy requires the development of a mental skill I would recommend that anyone who feels that they might ever need to use this technique should learn how to use it now.

If you drive a car a great deal and you think you may, at some time in the future, be in a situation where you will have to correct a skid then it obviously makes sense to attend a driving school where you can learn this skill. Waiting for the moment when your car starts to skid, and then deciding to learn, would obviously be less sensible.

* * *

That's my own very personal anti-cancer plan. I do not recommend it to you if you are suffering from cancer or if you are, at any time in the future, told that you have cancer. This is my own personal anti-cancer plan – designed to fit my beliefs and my philosophy of life. I would not follow any therapy in which I could not have faith. And I would make sure that I had faith in my chosen therapies. I have published my plan in the hope that it may help you think about how you would respond if you were told that you had cancer.

## 35 Understand Your Doctor

Any medical word that ends in '-ectomy' suggests a removal operation (as an 'tonsillectomy' or 'appendicectomy'). A word ending in '-otomy' suggests that an incision will be made (as in 'laparotomy' which means an incision in the abdomen). A word ending in '-plasty' suggests a plastic surgery operation (as in 'mammoplasty' which means a redesign of breast shape or size). A word ending in '-ostomy' means that an artificial hole has been made (as in 'colostomy' in which a hole is made in the colon) and the ending '-orrhaphy' means a repair (as in 'herniorrhaphy'). A word ending in '-oscopy' usually means having a look at something (as in 'bronchoscopy' which means having a look in the main tubes of the lungs and 'laparoscopy' which means taking a look inside the abdomen).

## 36   DON'T BE TRICKED INTO TAKING PILLS YOU DON'T WANT

For years now it has been common for nurses – both in hospitals and in nursing homes – to hide drugs in food and drink. Sedatives, tranquillisers and sleeping tablets are among the drugs most commonly abused in this way.

Now this despicable practice has been made legal in many countries. Nursing staff are officially allowed to crush pills patients don't want to take and to put them into food or drinks. The new rules allow nurses to trick children as well as adults in this way and cover private nursing homes as well as hospitals. To be frank, I would be less horrified if I heard that the authorities had announced that nurses would in future be allowed to steal from their patients whenever they felt it appropriate.

One recent study showed that 'thousands of care home residents were being prescribed powerful tranquillisers for minor problems to make life easier for staff.' Another study showed that more than a quarter of pensioners living in nursing homes are on powerful sedatives which have turned them into 'zombies'. This report concluded that elderly people living in care homes are nearly three times as likely to be given 'chemical cosh' drugs as those in the community. Elderly folk living in the community get mugged by their young neighbours. Elderly folk living in nursing homes get mugged by their nurses.

I believe that patients have a right to refuse drugs and that tricking them into taking products which may kill them (and which will very probably reduce their quality of life) is well outside the traditions of medical practice. It is, to be blunt, immoral and unethical.

Drugs are already wildly overused in hospitals and nursing homes and this advice legitimises a practice which reeks of state control. Whatever happened to human rights – let alone patient rights? It is no good for those defending the practice to say that hiding drugs in food and drink is already widespread. Rape and muggings are widespread. That doesn't make them acceptable.

If you suspect that the doctors and nurses looking after you might be tempted to give you medication without your consent give them a letter expressly forbidding them to give you drugs without your consent and insist that they all sign a note in which they promise not to do any such thing. I have no idea whether or not this would provide you with any legal protection but modern human rights legislation is so complex and far-reaching that I suspect that most doctors and nurses would not risk litigation by ignoring your specific instructions and their promise.

## 37 THE DANGER OF TOO MANY X-RAYS

For well over two decades I have been warning that doctors take far too many X-rays – and that since X-rays are known to be potentially hazardous these unnecessary investigations probably result in many unnecessary deaths.

It was back in 1895 that a fifty-year-old Professor of Physics in Germany made an accidental discovery which was to have as great an effect on the practice of clinical medicine and practical surgery as any other single technological step forward in the history of healing. His discovery has also become the most significant cause of cancer among the various different types of radiation to which most of us are exposed.

Professor Wilhelm Konrad von Röntgen was an experimental physicist and in 1895 he was investigating the effects of cathode rays. What caught his attention was the fact that, although the tube he was working with was covered with black cardboard, a greenish glow seemed to come from a piece of paper coated with a substance called barium platinocyanide which happened to be lying on a nearby bench. Röntgen realised that the paper must have been made luminous by some unknown rays – something other than the cathode rays he had started off investigating.

Röntgen decided to investigate further. He put a thousand page textbook between the tube and his piece of coated paper and found that the paper still became luminous.

Next, he placed his hand between the tube and the piece of paper and saw the bones of his hands appear on the luminous paper as dark shadows. His bones were obviously dense enough to prevent the flow of these unseen rays – rays which had gone straight through the soft tissues of his hand. He had discovered X-rays.

Doctors around the world soon saw the benefits to be obtained from Röntgen's discovery. At the end of February 1896, just under two months after Röntgen's original experiment, the British medical journal *The Lancet* published a report from Liverpool which described how a surgeon had used X-rays to help him localise an air-gun pellet before arranging for its removal.

By enabling doctors to see inside the living human body X-rays made it possible for physicians and surgeons to make much more accurate diagnoses than ever before.

Other research workers discovered that radioactive materials could be used to burn and destroy unwanted pieces of tissue. Doctors used X-rays to make the hair fall out from the heads of children so that their ringworm could be treated more effectively. More importantly, doctors found that radioactive materials could be used to attack cancerous growths. Pierre and Marie Curie were just two of the researchers who investigated the possibility of using radium as a therapeutic material in the early years of the twentieth century.

\* \* \*

By the beginning of the twentieth century the risks associated with X-rays had been well documented. A number of well-known researchers died during the early part of the century. But despite all this evidence X-rays were still used very widely. In the thirties and forties X-rays were used extensively to look for signs of tuberculosis in the lungs. The result of this was that years later a number of women who had been exposed to these heavy doses of X-rays developed breast cancer. By the 1950s it was clear that X-rays could cause a great deal of damage. (Though, as a boy in the 1950s, I remember that shoe shops often contained a device with which parents and shoe fitters could look at a foot inside a shoe to see that there was room for the foot to move. Like many other children I delighted in looking at my feet through this publicly available X-ray machine.)

By the 1970s doctors were beginning to worry that X-rays might be killing more people than they were saving. Mammography (X-rays of the breasts) had been introduced in the 1960s but doctors began to worry that mammography might be causing more cancer than it was detecting.

Doctors use X-rays in two main ways: as screening tools and as diagnostic aids. These two techniques together make up by far the largest exposure of artificial radiation to which most people are exposed. The average dose of X-ray used in a diagnostic X-ray is estimated to be about as dangerous as smoking six cigarettes. Every X-ray involves a risk and every unnecessary X-ray involves an unnecessary risk.

In my book *The Health Scandal* (first published in 1988) I concluded that most X-rays are entirely unnecessary. 'They are,' I wrote, 'potentially hazardous, they are extremely expensive and they are extremely unlikely to contribute anything to your doctor's knowledge of your illness.' The World Health Organisation has reported that X-rays can account for between six per cent and ten per cent of a country's expenditure on health.

One of the first papers to have been published criticising the number of X-rays done appeared in the *British Medical Journal* in the 1960s when a radiologist and a neurologist estimated that the consumption of X-ray film was doubling every thirteen years. The authors concluded that their study gave 'ample evidence that the great majority of plain X-ray films taken for such conditions as migraine and headache, did not contribute materially to the diagnosis.' They pointed out that much time and effort was wasted by doctors, radiographers and patients. Their plea for doctors to think before ordering X-rays fell on deaf ears.

In the 1970s the *British Medical Journal* again printed an appeal for doctors to order fewer X-ray pictures. By then it was estimated that the number of radiological examinations was increasing by ten per cent every year. This time the report in the BMJ pointed out that after routine chest X-rays were taken of 521 patients under the age of twenty, not one serious abnormality was detected.

By the 1980s the problem had become such an important one (and a global one) that the World Health Organisation issued a statement saying that 'routine X-ray examinations frequently are not worthwhile. Doctors,' said the W.H.O. 'ask for X-rays as a comforting ritual.' The W.H.O. went on to point out that X-rays are so overused and misused that they constitute a major source of population exposure to man-made ionizing radiation.

Today the situation continues to get worse. Many X-rays are done because patients demand them ('Couldn't you just do an X-ray to see what is causing the pain, doctor?' 'Wouldn't it be sensible to do an X-ray to make sure that nothing is broken?'). Doctors comply with these demands because they know that if they don't, and something subsequently goes wrong, then there is a real risk that a court will find them negligent. Taking an X-ray just-in-case is now commonplace and these days most X-rays are taken for legal rather than medical reasons. Some dentists do routine X-rays whenever they see their patients – apparently unaware that they may well be endangering their patients' lives.

The doctor or dentist who tells you that an X-ray is perfectly safe is a dangerous and uninformed fool.

Research has shown that in the USA the incidence of cancer rises in step with the number of doctors in an area. The over-enthusiasm of doctors for X-rays probably explains this. Three quarters of the current incidence of breast cancer in the United States is caused by earlier ionizing radiation, primarily from medical sources.

* * *

What can you do to protect yourself from unnecessary X-rays?

Before being X-rayed ask the doctor or dentist whether the X-ray is essential or simply routine.

Does the doctor suspect that something is wrong? Or is he merely taking the X-ray out of habit? Do you have any symptoms which suggest that an X-ray examination is necessary? Make the doctor (or dentist) think twice and he may decide that the X-ray isn't necessary after all.

And remember that many routine X-rays are simply taken because doctors know that if a patient ever takes them to court the lawyers will regard a failure to X-ray as a sign of incompetence and malpractice.

If a doctor or dentist looking after me confirmed that he was only taking an X-ray for legal reasons (and not because he expected the X-ray to help him decide how best to treat me) I would ask that he accept a short note, signed by me, confirming that I had rejected the offer of an X-ray.

X-rays were a great discovery. They can save lives. But they can also be another way in which your doctor can kill you.

## 38   BENZODIAZEPINE TRANQUILLISERS – FACTS EVERY PATIENT SHOULD KNOW

*'The world's biggest addiction problem is not teenagers taking hash but middle-agers taking sedatives. The tranquilliser is replacing tobacco. It will, perhaps, give us an even bigger problem. It may prove even more dangerous. Already Valium is said to be taken by 14 per cent of the population of Britain.'*

*'The habit usually starts insidiously. The patient may have a good excuse for taking a few tablets. A close friend or relative has died or there is a rush on at work. And the doctor finds it difficult to refuse the request for a little help.'*

*'The drugs which people take to help relieve their pressures vary. If he is young the addict may take drugs from a pusher. If he is older he may take drugs from a medical adviser.'*

That quote is taken from a book called *The Medicine Men* which I wrote and which was published way back in 1975.

\* \* \*

The benzodiazepine problem first began during the 1950s and 1960s when the type of problem being discussed in the doctor's consulting room changed. For the first time family doctors found that they were expected to deal with mental and psychological problems as well as physical problems. They were being consulted by patients who wanted comfort, support, encouragement and help with social and personal problems. As the link between stress and disease become better and better known so more and more patients went to their doctors wanting help with dealing with the stress in their lives.

But there was a big problem.

Doctors had never been trained to cope with psychological or stress induced problems. Most physicians had been taught more about tropical diseases than they had about anxiety or depression.

Doctors didn't know how to help these patients.

So, when the benzodiazepines were introduced and described as safe and effective drugs for the treatment of anxiety and a wide range of stress related disorders doctors welcomed the new pills with open arms. They prescribed them in huge quantities.

The result is that for many years the biggest drug addiction problem in the world has involved legally prescribed benzodiazepine tranquillisers and sleeping tablets which are widely and regularly prescribed for long periods for men, women and children suffering from stress and stress related symptoms.

It seems hard to believe but I first wrote about the dangers of tranquilliser addiction (and warned that doctors were overprescribing the drugs) back in 1973. Over the early years that I campaigned to get these drugs controlled more effectively I received tens of thousands of letters from tranquilliser addicts all over the world. In one month alone I counted over 6,000 letters about tranquillisers. It was the first time in my life that the mail arrived in huge grey mailbags.

After hundreds of articles and TV programmes my campaign to warn patients and doctors about the dangers of these drugs eventually forced the politicians to take action in Britain. (For 15 years I was abused and attacked by many members of the medical establishment who maintained that there were no problems.)

In 1988 – after 15 years of campaigning – doctors were warned of the hazards of handing out drugs such as diazepam, lorazepam, nitrazepam and temazepam for long-term use.

('Dr Vernon Coleman's articles, to which I refer with approval, raised concern about these important matters,' said Edwina Currie, British Parliamentary Secretary for Health, in the House of Commons in 1988. She was referring to the introduction of new controls relating to the prescribing of benzodiazepine tranquillisers.)

But not all doctors read official warnings. And not all governments followed Britain's example. And so tens of thousands of doctors are still handing out tranquillisers and sleeping tablets to millions of patients who have too much stress in their lives. In some developed countries over a third of the adult population is currently on prescribed tranquillisers, antidepressants or sleeping pills.

The simple truth is that the benzodiazepine tranquillisers can cause problems if they are taken for more than two weeks or so. Long-term use can cause all sorts of very real problems. And patients who have been taking the drugs for more than a week or two need to cut down slowly if they are to avoid withdrawal symptoms.

Sadly, it seems that doctors are addicted to the drugs too. Many doctors are still prescribing these damned pills by the lorry load. Occasionally, newspapers and magazines 'rediscover' the problem and publish articles about the huge addiction problem doctors have created.

\* \* \*

Here, for the record, are some facts about tranquillisers which many doctors still don't seem to know. Look at the dates carefully.

**Fact One**

In 1961, just a short time after chlordiazepoxide (the first widely prescribed benzodiazepine) had been introduced into clinical practice a report was written by three physicians from a hospital in California. Entitled 'Withdrawal Reactions from Chlordiazepoxide' the paper described very dramatically how patients who had been taking the drug suffered from withdrawal symptoms when the drug was stopped. The authors described how eleven patients who had been taking fairly high doses of chlordiazepoxide for up to six months were quite suddenly taken off the drug and given sugar tablets instead. Ten of the eleven patients experienced new symptoms or signs after the withdrawal of the chlordiazepoxide. Six patients became depressed, five were agitated and unable to sleep, two had major fits.

**Fact Two**

Testifying to a USA Senate Health sub committee in Washington in 1979 a psychiatrist claimed that patients could get hooked on diazepam in as little as six weeks. The same committee heard testimony that it is harder to kick the tranquilliser habit than it is to get off heroin.

**Fact Three**

In 1975 three doctors from the Drug Dependence Treatment Center at the Philadelphia VA Hospital and University of Pennsylvania, Philadelphia, published a paper in the *International Journal of the Addictions* entitled 'Misuse and Abuse of Diazepam: An Increasingly Common Medical Problem'. The three authors of the paper referred to papers published as far back as 1970 which had documented instances of physical addiction to chlordiazepoxide and diazepam and reported that since the end of 1972 they had noticed an increasing amount of diazepam misuse and abuse. Their paper concluded: 'All physicians should know that diazepam abuse and misuse is occurring and careful attention should be given to prescribing, transporting and storing this drug.'

**Fact Four**
In 1972 the *American Journal of Psychiatry* published a paper in which two doctors described how patients on diazepam had exhibited a cluster of symptoms which included tremulousness, apprehension, insomnia and depression. The patients had all been previously emotionally stable and the symptoms, which started suddenly, were quite severe. When these patients were taken off their diazepam their symptoms disappeared.

**Fact Five**
In 1968 the *Journal of the American Medical Association* described a series of eight patients who had been given diazepam. The patients became so depressed that seven of them had suicidal thoughts and impulses and two of them made serious attempts to commit suicide.

**Fact Six**
Several reports published in the 1960s and 1970s showed that the benzodiazepines seemed to increase hostility, aggressiveness and irritability. The benzodiazepines have also been associated with baby battering.

**Fact Seven**
In a paper published in 1979, researchers found a 'highly significant association between the use of minor tranquillisers and the risk of a serious road accident'. The conclusion was that a patient's risk of being involved in a serious accident was increased five fold if he or she was taking a benzodiazepine.

**Fact Eight**
Back in 1982 the Committee on Safety of Medicines advised doctors that the benzodiazepines should be prescribed for short periods only

and that withdrawal symptoms could be avoided by withdrawing medication slowly.

**Fact Nine**
When a 75-year-old lady was admitted to a British hospital in the early 1970s she was unable to walk or speak clearly and was confused and incontinent. She had been taking benzodiazepine sleeping tablets for a year. When her pills were stopped she made a physical recovery in three days.

\* \* \*

If you are hooked on a benzodiazepine tranquilliser or sleeping tablet you will need to wean yourself off your drug with care.

Here are some vital tips to help you.

1. Before doing anything visit your doctor and ask for his help. If he is unhelpful, if he tells you to cope by yourself or if he insists that you don't need to worry and that withdrawal is easy then I suggest that you find yourself a new doctor. If you see a doctor who tells you that the benzodiazepines never cause problems, don't cause addiction and can be stopped suddenly without danger my advice is simple: change doctors fast. There are plenty of good doctors around who understand the problem and who are prepared to help. Talk to friends and neighbours to find the name of a good local doctor.

2. You may experience unpleasant symptoms. The most common withdrawal symptoms include: tremor and shaking, intense anxiety, panic attacks, dizziness and giddiness, feeling faint, an inability to get to sleep and an inability to sleep through the night, an inability to concentrate, nausea, a metallic taste in your mouth, depression, headaches, clumsiness and poor coordination, sensitivity to light, noise and touch, tiredness and lethargy, a feeling of being 'outside your body', blurred vision, hot and cold feelings and a burning on your face, aching muscles, an inability to speak normally, hallucinations, sweating and fits.

3. Remember that you can minimise your symptoms by reducing your dose slowly. The rate at which you reduce your pills will depend upon the size of the dosage you have been taking and the length of time for which you have been on the pills.

4. Remember that the benzodiazepines cure nothing. But they do cover symptoms up. If you originally took your tablets for anxiety then the chances are that your original symptoms will return when you stop taking the tablets. Be prepared for this.

5. Warn your family and friends that you are likely to be going through a difficult time. Tell them what to expect and explain that you would welcome a little extra support, guidance, sympathy and patience. If you know someone else who wants to kick the habit then plan to do it together. Ring one another up, keep in touch, share your problems and keep your determination alive.

6. Do not try to give up these pills if you are going through a tricky patch at home or at work. Wait until things are more settled before you try to give up your pills.

7. Do not be tempted to try carving your tablets into tiny pieces. Break them into half by all means. But carving pills into fractions tends to make the whole procedure more difficult. It also makes everything more dramatic. Ask your doctor to prescribe the lowest dose of pills available so that you have the maximum amount of flexibility.

8. Do not despair if you reach a plateau and have difficulty in reducing your pills any more. Do not even despair if you have to increase your pills temporarily. You must stop these drugs at a rate that you find comfortable.

9. If you are taking a drug like lorazepam (which many experts believe is particularly difficult to come off) then your doctor may recommend that you substitute diazepam for part of the lorazepam and then cut down both drugs gradually. This *must* be done under medical supervision. Some people find that this helps cut down the withdrawal symptoms.

10. The question tranquilliser addicts ask most often is: 'How long does withdrawal last?'. And it is the question that causes most controversy. Some people are lucky. They can stop taking one of these drugs with relatively few – or even no – side effects. Others are less fortunate. Some experts claim that withdrawal should take no more than a few weeks. One expert I know says that it can last for 10 per cent of the time for which pills were taken. Some former addicts

claim that it has taken them years to get off their pills. The truth is that there is no fixed time for withdrawal. Some people can do it in days. Some take months.

'But,' say experts, 'it is important not to spread the withdrawal over too long a period.' If the pills are cut down too slowly then the patient will be taking the drug for longer than is necessary. 'The quicker you stop the pills,' the argument goes, 'the quicker you will recover. Spread the withdrawal over too long and your recovery will be slow.'

Patients sometimes respond to this by pointing out that although they cut down their pills in a matter of weeks they are still getting side effects months later.

But this does not necessarily mean that these side effects are withdrawal effects. It is important to remember that the benzodiazepines do not cure anything. If you were put on a tranquilliser ten years ago because you were feeling anxious and unhappy then the pills will have numbed your mind for ten years – but they will not have stopped your initial problem. When you stop the pills your anxiety will still be there. While you were taking the pills you may not have noticed the anxiety symptoms. If you were given your pills fifteen years ago to cover up the unhappiness of a bereavement then you will once more have to endure the unhappiness of that bereavement. The benzodiazepines will have put your emotions into a sort of pharmacological 'deep freeze'.

And, although the benzodiazepines do not cure anything they do numb the mind. They seal you off from the world and prevent you from experiencing the normal highs and lows of everyday life. Taking these drugs is like having your brain wrapped in a thick layer of cotton wool. While taking the drug you are immune to many of the pressures of everyday living; the world will be uniformly grey; you will be permanently anaesthetised.

Once you stop your pills your mind will suddenly be exposed to a whole range of stimuli. The anaesthetic will 'wear off' and you will 'wake up'. It can be a frightening experience. The world will suddenly appear a good deal brighter. Noises will seem louder and joys and sorrows will seem more acute. So, in addition to having to cope with old, half forgotten emotions you will find that your nerve endings are raw and easily stimulated.

Since all these symptoms occur immediately after stopping or cutting down the pills you will probably assume that the symptoms have developed because you have stopped your drug too quickly. I don't think that this is necessarily the case. The symptoms are an inevitable part of coming off tranquillisers but they may be there however slowly you reduce the dose. Extending the withdrawal period doesn't always affect the end result at all – it may merely prolong the agony.

Finally, it is essential that anyone planning to give up tranquillisers should spend a lot of time and effort learning how to relax and how to deal with stress. And remember: do not stop taking tranquillisers or sleeping tablets or try cutting down without getting professional help from your doctor.

*Note: In 1988, after my 15 year battle to persuade doctors and the establishment of the dangers of benzodiazepine tranquillisers, I predicted that the drug companies would attempt to deal with their reduced sales of tranquillisers by promoting antidepressants. The drug companies would, I warned, create a false need for antidepressants and would, within a few years, have replaced the tranquilliser problem with an antidepressant problem. That is exactly what happened.*

## 39  Lowering Blood Cholesterol

It isn't difficult to find many examples of the way that drug companies (and doctors) do their best to turn every illness into a profit making opportunity – while endangering the health of individual patients.

I believe that the treatment of raised blood cholesterol is one example.

For many years doctors and patients have believed that a patient who has a high blood cholesterol level may be more likely to suffer from heart trouble, high blood pressure or a stroke.

Vast amounts of money have been spent on screening patients for blood cholesterol levels. And many patients have been frightened half to death by finding out that their blood cholesterol levels are too high.

As a result, some years ago, the drug industry became excited by the prospect of introducing cholesterol lowering drugs on a large scale. Soon after they had first been introduced, drugs being prescribed to lower blood cholesterol were described as so safe and so effective that they would soon be prescribed for all individuals over the age of around 30 – whether or not they had a raised blood cholesterol level.

Drugs designed to lower blood fat and cholesterol levels have been on the market for some years now. Back in October 1992, I announced that in my view the latest drugs which looked like making a fortune for the drug industry were the products which were designed to lower blood cholesterol levels. At the same time I expressed scepticism about the value of these drugs – and concern about the possible hazards associated with their use.

When they were first launched the cholesterol lowering drugs were everybody's dream. The drug companies loved them because they knew that there was a massive, long-term international market. And many patients loved the idea of taking a pill to lower blood cholesterol because although they believed that a high cholesterol level meant a high heart attack risk many didn't want to stop eating the fatty foods that may cause a high blood cholesterol.

(Our 'pill for every ill' society sometimes still amazes me. I am constantly horrified at the number of people who know that their lifestyle is likely to result in a slow but early death but would still rather put all their trust into the greedy hands of the drug companies rather than doing something relatively simple and entirely risk free to help themselves.)

But there are several important questions to be answered here.

First, is a high blood cholesterol level really a danger sign?

The controversy over whether or not there is a direct link between a high blood cholesterol and the development of heart disease just won't go away. Most patients with heart disease have normal cholesterol levels and the alleged link between cholesterol levels and heart disease could, it seems, be a result of prejudices and assumptions being accepted as fact.

A Californian study couldn't find any link between high and low cholesterol levels and heart disease – but concluded that early deaths from heart disease are caused by other risk factors. A study of patients over the age of 70 failed to show any link between a high blood cholesterol level and any heart disease.

Second, is it wise to try and reduce a high blood cholesterol level?

Some trials have seemed to suggest that some of the patients who take cholesterol lowering drugs may be more rather than less likely to die.

Years ago a report in the *British Medical Journal* concluded that 'various studies have shown excess mortality from injuries and 'causes not related to illness' in those who have participated in trials in which their serum cholesterol concentration is lowered by either diet or drugs'.

A Swedish report looked into the possibility that a low cholesterol level may be linked to death from injury or suicide. They found that deaths from injuries, particularly suicide, were commoner in some men with a low blood cholesterol level.

An expert from the Cedars-Sinai Medical Center, Los Angeles, USA wrote an article in *The Lancet* which began: '...trials which have shown that the lowering of serum cholesterol concentrations in middle-aged subjects by diet, drugs or both leads to a decrease in coronary heart disease have also reported an increase in deaths due to suicide or violence. There has been no adequate explanation for this association.'

This expert suggested that a lowered serum cholesterol concentration may contribute to a: 'poorer suppression of aggressive behaviour'.

Californian researchers found that depression was much commoner among individuals who had a low blood cholesterol. They also found that the lower the cholesterol the more depressed the patient was likely to be.

A World Health Organisation trial of a drug designed to lower blood cholesterol levels reduced expectations that cholesterol lowering drugs might lower mortality from heart disease and raised new questions about the role of these drugs.

Does anyone really know for sure whether it is wise to reduce a high blood cholesterol level – or whether such action may create new and as yet poorly understood problems?

For women the truth seems even better hidden than it is for men. Research involving 15,000 women in Scotland showed that women who have high levels of cholesterol are less likely to die of heart disease than men who have high levels of cholesterol (even though the women had higher levels of cholesterol than the men).

The big (largely unasked) question is, of course: 'Can individuals reduce their chances of developing heart disease simply by eating more sensibly?'

This question is clearly of vital importance because if the answer is 'yes' then blood cholesterol levels (and cholesterol lowering drugs) become of academic, rather than practical, importance.

The curious and sad thing is that most doctors will, despite the 'first do no harm' philosophy which I have always regarded as a fundamental tenet of medical practice, be happy to reach for their pens and prescription pads, and dish out the pills, rather than bothering to ask themselves what is (or is not) a suitable diet for preventing heart disease.

In fact it *is* possible to cure heart disease without pills.

One of the basic cornerstones of this treatment programme is to follow a diet which cuts fat consumption down to somewhere between

10 per cent and 20 per cent – much lower in fat content than the usually recommended cholesterol lowering diet which is likely to contain 30 per cent fat.

Sadly, most doctors still prefer to stick with the advice handed out by slick suited drug company representatives – and to prescribe drugs rather than diet.

This is sad because depression and death aren't the only inconvenient side effects which may be associated with the use of cholesterol lowering drugs.

Other possible side effects known to be associated with just three of the many drugs commonly prescribed for the lowering of raised cholesterol levels may include: nausea, looseness of the bowels, impotence, headache, fatigue, drowsiness, skin rashes, pruritus, hair loss, weight gain, dizziness, cardiac arrhythmia and myositis-like syndrome (comprising myalgia, myopathy, muscle cramps and sometimes rhabdomyolysis), non-cardiac chest pain, vomiting, diarrhoea and abdominal pain, constipation, flatulence, asthenia, dyspepsia, muscle cramps, pancreatitis, paraesthesia, peripheral neuropathy, anaemia, hepatitis and hypersensitivity.

Remember, these are drugs which are prescribed to apparently healthy people – to keep them healthy without their having to give up burgers and cream doughnuts.

Are cholesterol lowering drugs effective? Will you live a longer, healthier, happier life if you take them?

Dunno.

Will you live a longer, healthier, happier life if you eat less and, in particular, cut your consumption of fatty foods?

I firmly believe so.

But where's the profit to be made out of advising patients to eat fewer burgers?

## 40   Ten Good Reasons Why You Shouldn't Trust Your Doctor

Here are a few excellent reasons why you should be extremely wary about your doctor. Remember that his motives (financial gain and professional status) may not be the same as yours (pain free survival).

1. He/she will have almost certainly been educated by drug companies anxious to sell their products – regardless of the side effects.

2. He/she may not know who you are – and may confuse you with someone else.

3. He/she may be using you as a guinea pig in a clinical trial. If your doctor gives you a packet of tablets (instead of a prescription) then the chances are high that he's being paid to test out a new drug.

4. He/she may well be sadly out of date. Most doctors are out of date within five years of leaving medical school.

5. He/she may be an alcoholic or a drug addict. Few professions turn to alcohol or drugs more often than doctors.

6. He/she probably has no idea what side effects may be associated with the drug he/she is prescribing.

7. He/she will almost certainly want to prescribe a drug for your symptoms – regardless of the fact that other methods of treatment may be both safer and more effective. Although providing drugs for patients suffering from chronic long-term problems (such as asthma, depression, high blood pressure or arthritis) is clearly a profitable area for pharmaceutical companies an even more profitable business is to sell drugs to perfectly healthy patients – the theory being that the drugs patients are given will stop them developing serious health

problems in the future. This is, I believe, an area where the drug companies are looking for huge growth in the future.

I predict that even if you are completely healthy, and look after yourself by eating sensibly, exercising regularly and controlling your stress exposure, there is still a very good chance that at some time during the next decade your doctor will try to persuade you to take a prescription drug – every day for the rest of your life.

8. He/she may be relying on test results which are wrong – or which he/she simply doesn't understand. Errors involving tests and investigations are much commoner than most patients (and most doctors) realise. Most tests aren't as reliable, as useful or as necessary as most people think.

9. He/she may be depressed and in no fit condition to make a diagnosis or prescribe treatment. Mental illness is commoner among doctors than almost any other group in our society.

10. He/she may make treatment decisions based on his/her own religious beliefs – even though those personal beliefs mean that you do not receive the most appropriate treatment. The doctor is unlikely to tell you that his/her decisions are being affected in this way.

## 41 THE BREAST CANCER SCANDALS

Few things illustrate the depths to which the modern medical profession has sunk better than the 'treatment' of breast cancer.

I was astonished and horrified when drug companies and doctors conspired to persuade completely healthy women to take a drug (tamoxifen) in order to try to prevent breast cancer despite the fact that it is known that the drug can cause cancer of the uterus. (As an aside, I know of one breast cancer patient whose doctors wanted her to take tamoxifen as a therapy. She declined their kind offer and put herself (very successfully) on a strict vegetarian diet. When she went to see her GP, after she had refused the tamoxifen, the GP's sole enquiry was: 'So, what will you do when you get cancer again?' The ignorance of some doctors is, I fear, matched only by their callousness and unsuitability for work within an 'allegedly' caring profession.)

But tamoxifen isn't the only so-called 'preventive' programme which I find it difficult to understand.

In recent years the failure of the 'cancer industry' to halt the incidence of breast cancer (or to find a cure) has resulted in what I believe is one of the most obscene aspects of modern medicine. Surgeons have started to remove perfectly healthy breasts from women in an attempt to prevent cancer developing. The theory is simple: if you remove a woman's breasts she cannot develop breast cancer.

This is not a new approach to breast cancer. Surgeons have been removing healthy breasts – as a method of preventing cancer – for nearly 20 years. But it is an approach which now seems to be winning a considerable amount of support. Some surgeons remove any woman's breasts. Others remove the breasts from women where there is a strong family history – and/or a genetic susceptibility to breast cancer.

I have several objections to the surgical removal of perfectly healthy breasts in an attempt to prevent breast cancer developing. First, any surgical operation carries a risk. Second, if a woman subsequently has breast enhancement surgery to replace breast tissue with silicone an old danger may be replaced by a new hazard. Third, a woman without breasts will not be able to breast feed and her babies will suffer. Fourth, where is this going to stop? Are we going to remove intestines to prevent bowel cancer? What about removing hearts to avoid heart attacks? Fifth, all this surgery will cost money – and one inevitable result of the utilisation of surgeons and hospital resources in this way will be that people who need urgent life-saving treatment won't get it. Finally, and most importantly, half of all breast cancer deaths could be avoided if women just cut down on fatty food and avoided meat.

I don't believe that removing healthy breasts or prescribing tamoxifen are the right way to tackle the epidemic of breast cancer now spreading throughout the western world.

The tragic truth is that the battle against breast cancer has so far been waged by an 'industry' (and the world wide anti-cancer establishment is now so large and so rich that it truly merits the word 'industry') which is in my view as corrupt and as incompetent as any other industry I can think of anywhere in the world.

For decades now the anti-cancer industry has offered women one ill thought out option after another. Surgeons around the world happily performed barbaric radical mastectomies (removing the whole breast and much of the tissue on the chest wall) even though the evidence showed that simply removing the breast lump would, for most women, provide an equal chance of success. The medical establishment has concentrated its efforts on surgery, radiotherapy and anti-cancer drugs not because these approaches offer patients the best hope but because the first two options provide work and wealth for doctors and hospitals and the third option offers wealth for doctors, hospitals and the pharmaceutical industry (of which the modern medical profession is, in truth, now little more than a marketing arm.)

Women have been discouraged from examining their own breasts (even though self-examination produces good results) and encouraged to attend mammography clinics (even though the value of such clinics is questionable and many doctors now agree with my long held fear that regularly X-raying breasts might actually cause cancer). Why?

Could it be that when a woman examines her own breasts no one makes any money but when a woman attends a mammography clinic there is more work and more money for the medical establishment? How can a once a year (or once every few years) visit to a mammography clinic possibly provide the same level of protection as a once a month manual check-up at home?

## 42 | Questions To Ask Your Surgeon

Here are the questions you should ask the doctor if you need to go into hospital for surgery:

1.  How often do you perform operations of this type? (And how long have you been doing them?)
2.  How long do you expect the operation to take?
3.  What are the possible complications?
4.  Where will you need to cut? How long will the cut be?
5.  Do you expect that I will need a drain, a drip or a catheter after the operation?
6.  How soon after surgery will I be able to start eating and drinking?
7.  What pain relief do you expect me to need? Will I have to ask for this or will it be provided automatically?
8.  How long will I need to stay in bed?
9.  When will I be able to have a bath (or shower)?
10. When will I be able to resume normal activities such as driving or sex?
11. When will I be able to start playing sport again?
12. When will you need to see me after I leave the hospital?
13. How long am I likely to be in hospital?

When you go into hospital remember to take with you notebooks and pencils (to jot down questions you want to ask doctors and/or nurses and to make a note of their answers).

## Note 1

If nurses, doctors and administrators call you by your first name return the compliment. It is disrespectful and demeaning for hospital staff to address patients by their first names when they do not themselves expect to be addressed in that way.

## Note 2

Anyone who calls a patient a 'client' rather than a patient should be ignored. Clients are people who consult lawyers and social workers and who buy cars and fridges. People who are ill are patients.

## Note 3

Patients having surgery invariably (and reasonably) want to know when they will be fit to resume work, household duties and sex. These queries (often unasked) are entirely reasonable. I am, however, constantly surprised by the fact that doctors, when patients ask them how long it will be before they are fit to start work again, will frequently offer a single fixed time scale. It is clearly absurd to tell a professional wrestler that he will be fit for work at the same time as a librarian or a telephone operator. And, of course, the health and general fitness of the individual patient has a tremendous impact on the time needed for a full recovery. The only thing a doctor can do is predict functionality. And even that has to be pretty vague. So, when you ask how long it will be before you are fit to start work explain what your work entails – or ask a general question (such as when will I be fit to walk down the garden, play golf, play tennis) which will give you an idea of the answer you want. If that fails try another doctor – explain exactly what you have to do for a living, and make sure that he or she knows exactly what your operation entailed.

## 43 | How To Read Your Prescription

When writing out a prescription many doctors still use abbreviations derived from a rough and ready version of Latin. The abbreviations are used to give instructions to the pharmacist who will turn the prescription into a bottle of pills. Occasionally, pharmacists may forget to put these instructions onto the label, so it is useful for patients to be able to read their prescriptions themselves. Here are some of the commonest abbreviations – and their meanings:

ac – before meals
alt die – alternate days
bd (or bid) – twice a day
c – with
dol urg – when the pain is severe
gutt – drops
hs – at bedtime
m – mix
om – every morning
on – every evening
prn – when needed
qd (or qid) four times a day
r – take
sig – label
sos – if necessary
stat – immediately
td (or tid or tds) – three times a day
ung – ointment

## 44 | How To Get The Best Out Of Your Doctor

Here are five tips designed to help you make sure that you get the best out of your doctor (and every other doctor who treats you) – and minimise your chances of being made ill by a doctor.

### 1. Take A Positive Interest In Your Own Health
Patients used to hand over their health (and their lives) to their doctors – without ever questioning what was happening to them. That is a dangerous way to live these days. Patients used to rely on being able to see the same doctor pretty much throughout their lives. They got to know his strengths and weaknesses. And, most important, patient and doctor grew to know and trust one another. These days the patient who sees the same doctor three times running can think him or herself lucky. If you need a doctor out of hours the chances of seeing someone you know are slim indeed.

Patients who take an interest in their own health may sometimes feel that the doctors and nurses who are looking after them regard them as a nuisance. But all the evidence shows clearly that such patients get better quicker, suffer fewer unpleasant side effects and live longer than patients who simply lie back passively and allow the professionals to take over. Be a difficult patient – you'll live longer. If your doctor wants you to take a drug (and all pills, tablets, capsules, medicines, potions, creams and so on are drugs) make sure you know what to expect. Who is going to benefit most? You? Your doctor? Or the drug company? If your doctor wants you to have surgery then make sure that you know what the surgery entails, what the possible consequences might be and what the alternatives are. Good questions to ask your doctor are: 'Would you have this operation if you were me?' or: 'Would you recommend this operation to someone in your close family?'

Always remember that doctors do some very silly things – mainly because they never really think about what they are doing (or question their own traditions). For example, psychiatrists invariably put all the depressed patients together in one room. The result of this is that the depressed patients become even more depressed. And psychiatrists (and psychologists) describe patients as suffering from agoraphobia when in fact they are nervous about going out and meeting other people (sociophobia) rather than going into wide open spaces. (Stupidity and a blind allegiance to unsupportable traditions are not traits exhibited exclusively by psychiatrists.)

## 2. Don't Be Afraid To Ask For A Second Opinion

Telling your doctor that you want a second opinion will probably take a great deal of courage. Many doctors are sensitive creatures – they may show their hurt if their all-knowingness is questioned. But just remember that the stakes are high. Your life is at stake. (And, if there is time, don't be afraid to check out the past record of the doctor who is going to treat you. One surgeon working in a hospital may have a survival rate which is twice as good as another surgeon working in the same hospital. If you allow the less competent surgeon to operate on you then your chances of walking out of the hospital may be halved. Those are odds you cannot and should not ignore.)

## 3. Remember Coleman's First Law Of Therapy

If you develop new symptoms while receiving medical treatment then the chances are that the new symptoms are caused by the treatment you are receiving. Doctors do not like accepting that the treatments they recommend can do harm. It reminds them that they are mortal and fallible. But don't just ignore it if you develop a rash, indigestion, tinnitus, a headache or some other side effect: report it to your doctor straight away. Don't stop medication without asking his advice first. Some side effects are mild and if the drug is working and helping to control or defeat a serious or life-threatening condition then the side effects may be of little consequence. But other side effects may kill. Many of the thousands who die each year could still be alive if they had taken action earlier when side effects started. Remember, too, that doctors are notoriously reluctant to admit that their therapy could be making you ill. This is partly through ignorance (doctors don't often bother to read drug company information sheets), partly through a fear of litigation (the doctor may be frightened that if he admits that his treatment has made you ill he will receive a letter from your lawyer) and partly through a natural human unwillingness to admit responsibility for something that has gone wrong (this brand of unwillingness is unusually well-developed among doctors who are encouraged to think of themselves as godlike by many of their other more passive patients).

### 4. Always Study All The Options:
There are very few truly holistic practitioners around. But there is nothing at all to stop you being a holistic patient. For example, if your doctor tells you that you need surgery ask him how long you have got before you need to make a decision – and then use that time to make sure that you assess all the possible options. When you are trying to choose between orthodox medicine, acupuncture, homoeopathy, osteopathy or whatever make a list of all the advantages and disadvantages of every available type of therapy – and every available practitioner. Look at the claims and the potential side effects of each therapy and ask each practitioner to tell you where you can find out more. Never forget that you are unique – and that your condition requires a unique solution.

### 5. Constantly Acquire Information
Information is the key to success in any field. If you want to be a successful investor then you need access to good information. You must know where to obtain information and you must know how to understand it. Exactly the same is true of health. In order to stay healthy – and regain good health if you fall ill – you must have access to good information. Only when you have the best information will you know what questions to ask and how to understand the answers. Doctors (and indeed many others in the health business) are notoriously bad at communicating – even though doctor-patient communication is of vital importance. Since doctors don't seem keen to bridge the understanding gap between patients and themselves it is up to you to make the effort. If you have a long-term health problem then learn as

much as you can about the disorder and all the possible types of treatment available. I have met patients with chronic health disorders (such as diabetes, arthritis, high blood pressure and so on) who know more about their condition than their doctors. Which patients do you think do best – those who know a great deal about their condition or those who know next to nothing? It may sound cynical to point out that countries are no longer run by governments but by drug, arms, chemical and oil companies but it isn't. It is simply a truth that you should remember. Doctors should do more to defend and protect their patients but, sadly, most are now simply paid up members of a medical establishment which has sold itself to the pharmaceutical industry. In my first book (*The Medicine Men*), published in 1975, I pointed out that doctors have become little more than a marketing arm of the drug companies. I was laughed at when I said it. But I wonder how many people would still think it funny.

Doctors and nurses often moan that patients complain too much – and ask too many questions. Not true. The vast majority of patients complain far too little – and ask far too few questions. Asking questions (and making your needs understood and respected) will help you, and other patients, live longer, healthier lives. Information is the most valuable resource on earth – far more valuable than gold or platinum if you know what to do with it when you get it. Accurate information gives power to those who have it. Information gives you power over many things but most important of all it gives you power over your own health – and increases your chances of survival in an increasingly dangerous and dishonest world.

There is, of course, plenty of information available. The world is, indeed, awash with information. Have you ever wondered how you can possibly keep up? Have you ever worried about what to read and, more importantly, who to believe? How can you possibly keep up with the knowledge flow – particularly when having the right information is so crucial; literally a matter of life and death?

The problem is made worse by the fact that there are many lobbyists and PR organisations busy laying traps and false information in order to sell specific products and particular points of view. For financial reasons these people often want to hide the truth from you. Much of the material you read in newspapers and magazines has been 'planted' by public relations experts – wanting to sell or protect a particular product. The same is true of TV and radio programmes. There are just as many spin doctors in the world of health care as there are in politics.

How do you differentiate between the commercially inspired hype and the truth? In our society those who shout the loudest (and have the biggest bank balances) are invariably the ones who get most of the attention – regardless of their real value. You must learn to differentiate between the good and the bad.

Do be wary about trusting what you read in newspapers, magazines and even books. The quality of writing on health matters these days is appalling. A surprising number of publications seem to publish press releases and handouts rather than critical assessments. Many 'health writers' have little or no training and no ability at all to 'read' a scientific paper. Most are easily 'conned'.

When I was making a programme about the use of animals in drug research I wanted to reveal that a large charity had been using dogs in its experiments – despite having denied this. The BBC producer rang me and told me that we couldn't use the item. Her reason? A public relations officer for the charity had assured her that the charity hadn't used any dogs – only dog tissue. (When I asked the producer where she thought the dog tissue came from she seemed genuinely surprised at the notion that it might have been necessary to kill dogs in order to obtain the dog tissue.)

Most medical journalists don't know what questions to ask and wouldn't have the courage to ask them even if they did. Many of the doctors who write for the press are unwilling to criticise the establishment or the pharmaceutical industry. In the end, it's all down to whom you trust. And that's a choice you must make.

### Coleman's Laws
Here are ten Coleman's laws to help you get the best out of your doctor:
1.  If you develop new symptoms while receiving treatment then the chances are the new symptoms are caused by the treatment.
2.  Never trust a doctor who tells you that the drug he is prescribing is free of all side effects.
3.  There is no such thing as minor surgery.
4.  Assume your doctor wants to kill you. You will live longer.

5. When your doctor hands you a packet of pills to 'save you going to the pharmacy' you are probably being used as a guinea pig and helping to test a new drug.

6. Before accepting a vaccination ask your doctor to confirm that the vaccine can do you no harm. There is no point in taking something which can kill you if you are well.

7. If your doctor wants you to have tests done ask him how the results will affect your treatment. If they won't have any effect then the tests are not worth having.

8. Ask your doctor if a drug is really necessary if your symptoms are merely irritating. Drugs can kill.

9. If you visit a surgeon the chances are that he will want to operate. Visit a physician with the same symptoms and he may want to give you pills. Remember: surgeons operate and physicians hand out pills; it's what they do.

10. Drug side effects only appear after time. The big advantage of a drug which has been around for years is that it is unlikely to be the world's most dangerous drug. The longer a drug has been around the more we will know about it.

## AFTERWORD

*When an edition of my book 'How To Stop Your Doctor Killing You' was first published in China I was asked to write a special foreword. In the belief that it might be of some interest to Western readers I have included it here:*

Foreword to the Chinese Edition of *How To Stop Your Doctor Killing You*

As modern, drug-reliant Western so-called orthodox medicine spreads into China the public relations departments of the huge international drug companies will work overtime to convince practitioners and patients that modern, powerful, Western drugs (manufactured in such countries as America, Britain, Switzerland, Germany and France) are the only effective way to prevent and combat disease.

The medical profession will, in general, support and work with the drug companies to promote the belief that the best way to prevent or to cure illness is to take a drug.

In Europe and the United States of America the drug companies now control the medical profession. To a large extent doctors have become the marketing arm of the pharmaceutical industry.

Western doctors may be members of a profession which has a long, proud history but during the last century many doctors in the USA and Europe have sold their soul and their honour to the drug companies.

* * *

Drugs can be useful, of course. Used wisely and with caution drugs can, and do, save lives. And the Western trained, twenty-first century physician can do a great deal of good.

But what the medical establishment and the international

pharmaceutical companies will not tell you is that drugs which can cure can also kill. Drugs can, and do, cause a great deal of harm.

An astonishing one in six patients in American and European hospitals are there because they have been made ill by a doctor. And most of those patients were made ill by drugs.

Iatrogenesis – the name used to describe the phenomenon of doctor-induced illness – is now one of the three biggest causes of illness and death in Europe and the USA. Doctor-induced illness now ranks alongside cancer and heart disease. Every year hundreds of thousands of patients are made ill or even killed by the doctors to whom they entrusted their health. And drugs are responsible for the largest part of this epidemic of doctor-induced death and disease.

Drugs and doctors can do both good and harm.

The secret of survival is to know how to get the best out of both doctors and drugs; to know how to use them to your advantage; and to know where and how to fit them both safely into an effective, long-term programme of self-preservation.

And that is what this book, *How To Stop Your Doctor Killing You*, is all about.

*Professor Vernon Coleman MB ChB DSc, England, September 2002*

*'I speak the truth not as much as I would, but as much as I dare and I dare a little more as I grow older.'*

MONTAIGNE

Also by Vernon Coleman

# Bodypower
The secret of self-healing

A new edition of the sensational book which hit the *Sunday Times* bestseller list and *The Bookseller* Top Ten Chart.

This international bestseller shows you how you can harness your body's amazing powers to help you cure nine out of ten illnesses without seeing a doctor.

The book also covers:

- How to use bodypower to stay healthy
- How your personality affects your health
- How to stay slim for life
- How to break bad habits
- How to relax your body and mind
- How to improve your figure
- And much much more!

*'Don't miss it. Dr Coleman's theories could change your life.'*
(Sunday Mirror)

*'A marvellously succinct and simple account of how the body can heal itself.'*
(The Spectator)

*'Could make stress a thing of the past.'*
(Woman's World)

*'There are plenty of good books on heath care in the shops and for starters I'd recommend "Bodypower" by Dr Vernon Coleman which shows you how to listen to your body and understand its signals.'*
(Woman's Own)

*'... one of the most sensible treatises on personal survival ever published ... It sets out an enormous amount of knowledge in the easiest possible way.'*
(Yorkshire Evening Post)

Paperback £9.95
Published by European Medical Journal
Order from Publishing House • Trinity Place • Barnstaple • Devon
EX32 9HJ • England
Telephone 01271 328892 • Fax 01271 328768
www.vernoncoleman.com

Also by Vernon Coleman

# Spiritpower

Discover your spiritual strength

- Find out who you are (and what you want)
- Three words that can change your life
- How to get what you want out of life
- Use your imagination and your subconscious mind
- Why you have more power than you think you have
- How you can control your own health
- Why you shouldn't be afraid to be a rebel
- How to stand up for yourself
- Know your fears and learn how to conquer them

What the papers say about *Spiritpower*:

'*The final tome in his trilogy which has produced the bestsellers "Bodypower" and "Mindpower", this is Dr Coleman's assessment of our current spiritual environment, and his prescriptions for change. He advises both awareness and rebellion, recommending ways to regain personal autonomy and fulfilment.*'
(The Good Book Guide)

'*"Spiritpower" will show you how to find freedom and give meaning to your life.*'
(Scunthorpe Evening Telegraph)

'*This is a handbook for tomorrow's revolutionaries. Dr Coleman offers an understanding of the society we live in, in order to show where our freedom was lost.*'
(Greenock Telegraph)

Paperback £12.95
Published by European Medical Journal
Order from Publishing House • Trinity Place • Barnstaple • Devon
EX32 9HJ • England
Telephone 01271 328892 • Fax 01271 328768
www.vernoncoleman.com

Also by Vernon Coleman

# Food For Thought

Between a third and a half of all cancers may be caused by eating the wrong foods. In this best-selling book Dr Coleman explains which foods to avoid and which to eat to reduce your risk of developing cancer. He also lists foods known to be associated with a wide range of other diseases including asthma, gall bladder disease, headaches, heart trouble, high blood pressure, indigestion and many more.

Years of research have gone into the writing of this book which explains the facts about mad cow disease, vegetarian eating, microwaves, drinking water, food poisoning, food irradiation and additives. It contains all the information you need about vitamins, carbohydrates, fats and proteins plus a list of 20 superfoods which Dr Coleman believes can improve your health and protect you from a wide range of health problems. The book also includes a "slim-for-life" programme with 48 quick slimming tips to help you lose weight safely and permanently.

' ... *a guide to healthy eating which reads like a thriller*'
(The Good Book Guide)

'*Dr Vernon Coleman is one of our most enlightened, trenchant and sensible dispensers of medical advice*'
(The Observer)

'*I consider it to be one of the most brilliant books of its kind that I have ever read. Not only are the contents a mine of information and advice but the style is such that it makes the whole book so thoroughly enjoyable to read; indeed it is a book difficult to put down.*'
(G.P., Streatham)

'*His no nonsense approach to all foods makes finding your way through the nutritional maze that much easier.*'
(Evening Times)

Paperback £12.95
Published by European Medical Journal
Order from Publishing House • Trinity Place • Barnstaple • Devon
EX32 9HJ • England
Telephone 01271 328892 • Fax 01271 328768
www.vernoncoleman.com

Also by Vernon Coleman

# Superbody

A healthy immune system won't simply protect you against infection – it will also prove to be an essential factor in your body's ability to fight off all other diseases – including cancer.

The first two parts of this book explain why and how our bodies are under siege – and why the incidence of cancer and infectious diseases is rising rapidly (and likely to continue rising).

Infectious diseases started to become resistant to antibiotics a quarter of a century ago. Since then the situation has steadily worsened, and it is now probably too late for the medical profession to reverse the situation. Infectious diseases are coming back in a big way and the incidence of cancer is also going to continue to rise.

And so the third part of *Superbody* explains how you can protect yourself against these, and other threats, by improving the strength, efficiency and effectiveness of your immune system.

- How to boost your immune system
- How to increase your resistance to infection and disease
- How to protect yourself against cancer
- The best 101 foods in the world
- Improve your mental health
- How to spot early warning signs of disease
- How to de-stress your mind and body
- How to avoid environmental risks
- And much, much more

*'A helpful and informative read for those who have been swept up by the lifestyle and excesses of the 20th/21st century.'*
(Evening Chronicle)

Paperback £9.95
Published by European Medical Journal
Order from Publishing House • Trinity Place • Barnstaple • Devon
EX32 9HJ • England
Telephone 01271 328892 • Fax 01271 328768
www.vernoncoleman.com

Also by Vernon Coleman

# The Story of Medicine

Subtitled "An account of the social, political, economic and military influences on the health of the people and the practice of medicine from the beginning of time to the modern period", this book covers the development of medicine and medical practice from the early days of Mesopotamia through to the present day. Full of fascinating anecdotes which really bring the past to life. Contents include:

- The power of the Gods
- Our debt to the Orient
- The great men of Greece
- The Roman legacy
- The Arabian influence
- The first medical schools
- The Black Death
- Drugs and the drug industry
- Quackery and genius
- Women in medicine

*"'The Story of Medicine" endeavours to chart the history of medicine from man's origins to the present day in 250 pages. Vernon Coleman manages to handle this project with aplomb. The book concerns itself with the more social and political aspects of medicine, and the main historical thread is broken up by an abundance of anecdotes and amusing stories about dodgy quacks... it will sell by the bucket-load because (it is) a very worthwhile read.'*
(The Leader)

*'...accessible and very readable.'*
(Huddersfield Examiner)

Paperback £12.95
Published by European Medical Journal
Order from Publishing House • Trinity Place • Barnstaple • Devon
EX32 9HJ • England
Telephone 01271 328892 • Fax 01271 328768
www.vernoncoleman.com

For a catalogue of Vernon Coleman's books
please write to:

Publishing House
Trinity Place
Barnstaple
Devon EX32 9HJ
England

Telephone      01271 328892
Fax            01271 328768

*Outside the UK:*
Telephone      +44 1271 328892
Fax            +44 1271 328768

*Or visit our website:*

www.vernoncoleman.com